SAVAGE STICKER BOOK

TERRY DEARY

SCHOLASTIC

Scholastic Children's Books,
Euston House, 24 Eversholt Street,
London, NW1 1DB, UK

A division of Scholastic Ltd
London ~ New York ~ Toronto ~ Sydney ~ Auckland
Mexico City ~ New Delhi ~ Hong Kong

Published by Scholastic Ltd, 2008

Some of the material in this book has previously been published in
Horrible Histories: The Rotten Romans, The Ruthless Romans, The Awesome Ancient Quiz Book, The Vicious Vikings, The Angry Aztecs, Dark Knights and Dingy Castles, The Terrible Tudors, Even More Terrible Tudors, Cruel Crime and Painful Punishment and The Slimy Stuarts

ISBN 978 1407 10534 5

Printed and bound by Tien Wah Press Pte. Ltd, Malaysia

2 4 6 8 10 9 7 5 3 1

Additional text by Jenny Siklos, Pam Kelt, Dereen Taylor and Stuart Branch
Additional illustrations and colour work by Stuart Martin, Mike Phillips and Jon Darron
Activities created and produced by The Complete Works, St Mary's Road, Royal Leamington Spa, Warwickshire, CV31 1JP, UK

Contents

ROTTEN ROMAN RULERS

Rome began as a group of villages in Italy. First there were Roman 'kings' – but they were thrown off their thrones for being too wicked. Then the people decided to rule themselves – that's called a 'republic'. They elected leaders called consuls. The last consul, mighty Julius Caesar, was murdered and his adopted son became the first Roman emperor, Augustus. Now the Romans were ready to become one of the world's largest empires.

Rome had its fair share of rotten rulers. Here are a few foul facts about them. Some of the words have been left out. Add the word stickers to complete the sentences.

1) TIBERIUS (AD 14 – 37) SAID THAT HE WOULD ______ THE ______ OF ANYONE WHO DISOBEYED HIM.

2) CALIGULA (AD 37 – 41) WANTED SOMEONE TO HELP HIM TO ______ SO HE GAVE THE JOB TO HIS ______

3) CLAUDIUS (AD 41 – 54) HAD HIS ______ EXECUTED.

4) NERO (AD 54 – 68) TRIED TO ______ HIS ______

5) VITELLIUS (AD 69) HAD HIS ______ THROWN IN THE ______ IN ROME.

6) ANTONIUS (AD 138 – 161) DIED OF ______ TOO MUCH ______

7) ELIOGABALUS (AD 218 – 222) HAD THE CURIOUS HOBBY OF COLLECTING EVERY ______ HE COULD FIND.

8) HONORIUS (AD 395 – 423) HAD A ______ CALLED 'ROME'.

Julius Caesar was a brilliant Roman consul. But when he became too big for his boots, his number was up. There was just one way to get rid of him – assassination. Many of the assassins wounded each other as they fought to stick so many knives into one body! Caesar received twenty-three wounds. Spot ten bloody differences between the two pictures and circle them with a pencil.

Augustus Caesar was a very good emperor … so the Romans thought it was a good idea to have more of them. But even when some bad, mad and sad men became emperors, the Romans didn't give up on the idea – they just murdered the man and got a new one! Here are some weird emperor facts. Work out which ones are TRUE or FALSE and add the correct stickers.

1) You could be executed for saying the word 'goat' near Caligula.

2) A doctor saved Claudius from poisoning by making him vomit with a feather.

3) Nero played the fiddle and watched while Rome burned.

4) Commodus enjoyed shooting the heads off ostriches with his bow and arrow.

5) Gordian hanged himself with his shoelaces.

6) Eliogabalus made his ministers carry sheep guts to the temple as a gift for the gods.

GRUESOME GAMES

It wasn't just the Roman emperors who were rotten. The people were pretty nasty, too! Murder was made into a 'sport'. Men and women were killed for fun. The idea of fighting and killing as a game probably began at funerals…

People believed that the souls of the dead were kept happy with human blood, so they sacrificed prisoners of war or slaves at funerals. But it was more fun to watch those victims fight for their lives. The funeral fights became so popular that they were moved out of graveyards and into huge arenas. The greatest arena was the Colosseum in Rome. This arena held 50,000 bloodthirsty Romans. Look carefully and work out which of the numbered pictures below are part of the Colosseum.

Fighters became known as gladiators. Gladiators weren't all the same. There were all sorts of different types. Read the description of each gladiator. Then add the correct picture sticker.

ANDABATAE
Fought blindfolded – very funny for the audience.

SAGITTARII
Fought with bows and arrows – hoping for an arrow escape.

RETIARII
Fought with nets and a trident – a bit fishy that.

DIMACHERI
Fought with two swords – slick slicers.

SECUTORES
Fought with sword and shield – they were lucky ones.

LAQUEATORES
Fought with a rope – no noose was bad news for them.

Gladiators wore armour to protect themselves when fighting – a GALEA (helmet with a visor), a GALERUS (metal shoulder piece), a MANICAE (leather bands on elbow or wrist) and an OCREA (shin guard of metal or boiled leather). They also used different weapons – a FASCINA (harpoon), a GLADIUS (sword), a HASTA (lance), an IACULUM (net), a PARMA (round shield), a SCUTUM (large oblong shield) and a SICA (curved sword). Find the words in CAPITALS above in the wordsearch. The words are written across, up, down, diagonally, forwards or backwards.

H	I	A	P	A	R	M	A
A	S	U	I	D	A	L	G
S	V	A	T	H	U	F	A
T	B	N	A	E	L	A	G
A	Y	I	O	C	Q	S	O
O	T	C	J	F	I	L	C
C	G	S	E	A	M	S	R
R	M	A	N	I	C	A	E
E	H	F	L	U	R	A	C
A	O	C	T	E	P	I	T
A	T	U	L	N	R	A	C
T	M	A	N	X	A	U	I
I	A	C	U	L	U	M	S

DID YOU KNOW…?

If a gladiator wasn't quite dead, a servant would finish him with a hammer blow to the head.

FEARSOME FIGHTERS

Gladiators were not the only ones to fight in the arenas. Criminals did as well. They dressed like gladiators but the Romans knew they were not the real things. Those criminals (called 'noxii') gave the Romans all the blood and death they wanted to see and they were cheap. The real gladiators cost a lot of money to feed and train. Gladiators were not cheap slaves to be wasted.

Not everyone thought that killing people for fun was a great day out. The Roman writer, Seneca, went to see the Roman games and saw the 'noxii', doomed to die. Add the missing word stickers to find out what he wrote…

I HAPPENED TO DROP IN ON THE MIDDAY ______ IN THE ARENA. I WAS LOOKING FOR A LITTLE ENTERTAINMENT BUT SAW ONLY BUTCHERY, PURE AND SIMPLE. THE ______ HAVE NOTHING TO PROTECT THEM. THEIR ______ ARE OPEN TO EVERY BLOW, AND EVERY BLOW FINDS ITS MARK. THEY ARE LASHED FORWARD SO THEY CAN'T ______ THE SWORD. IN THE MORNING MEN FIGHT LIONS AND BEARS, AT NOON THEY FIGHT EACH OTHER. THE WINNERS FIGHT AGAIN AND AGAIN UNTIL THEY ARE ______ DEATH IS THE FIGHTER'S ONLY WAY OUT. THE SPECTATORS SAY, 'BUT THESE MEN ARE HIGHWAY ROBBERS AND ______. THEY DESERVE ALL THAT THEY ARE GETTING!' CAN'T YOU SEE HOW ______ THIS SPORT IS?

Gladiators were supposed to fight hard and put on a good show for the audience. But one group shocked Emperor Caligula when they refused to fight. Put the missing picture stickers in the right order to find out what happened...

1	2	3	4
5	6	7	8

Caligula called it 'murder' and he probably had the Retiarii executed anyway. But at least they must have had a bit of a chuckle before they died!

Want some fun in ancient Rome? Then get an animal to fight against a gladiator or against another animal. Even if the animal won, hunters or dogs then killed them. But some animals became favourites of the crowd. They fought bravely and the crowd decided they should live. One rhinoceros fought so well the crowd loved it. The rhino fought time and again in the arena for emperors Titus and Domitian. Work out which small picture matches the big one in the middle.

ROTTEN ROMAN ARMY

The Roman army was nasty, cruel and vicious. That's why they won a lot of fights. If you are a soldier and you surrender, you might expect your enemy to spare your life. Not if the enemy was a Roman. And the Romans didn't just kill their prisoners – they took them back to Rome and killed them in the city centre so the rest of the Romans could watch.

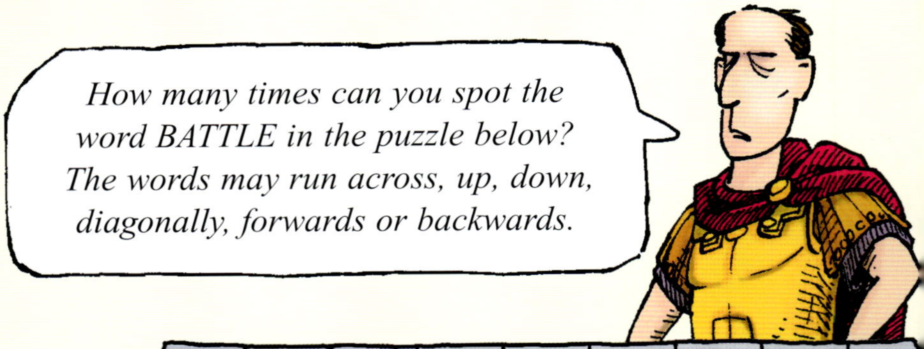

To conquer another country wasn't easy. Battles were fierce and many soldiers were injured. An army doctor had to amputate mangled limbs and mend broken bones. Help this wounded soldier get back out on the battlefield. Add the stickers of his armour and weapons.

B	A	T	T	L	E	T	A	B
A	E	L	T	T	A	B	B	B
T	A	T	L	L	B	A	A	E
T	L	E	T	B	A	T	T	L
L	T	T	A	L	T	T	T	T
E	L	T	T	L	T	L	L	T
T	E	T	E	A	L	E	E	A
T	E	L	T	T	B	L	A	B
A	L	A	T	A	A	T	T	E
B	A	B	E	T	B	T	B	L
A	A	L	A	A	A	A	A	T
T	T	L	T	T	A	B	T	T
T	T	T	A	B	T	B	T	A
L	L	A	L	B	T	L	L	B
E	E	B	A	T	T	L	E	E
B	A	E	L	T	T	A	B	B

When the Romans captured New Carthage in Spain in 202 BC, the soldiers were ordered to kill everyone. The soldiers did more than that – they cut the legs off animals and chopped dogs in two. Picture it: chopped chows to the left, poodle pieces to the right and halved hounds h'everywhere. Find the stickers to piece the poor pooches back together.

You did not want to be an enemy of Rome. If you were, Roman soldiers made you suffer … and suffer … and then suffer some more. Read about the Roman army's rotten antics and add the correct picture stickers to the facts.

1) Some Roman soldiers who rebelled against Rome were tied to stakes and whipped. Then the backs of their necks were chopped with an axe. They weren't beheaded completely.

2) In AD 214, 370 soldiers were thrown from the Tarpeian Rock in Rome for deserting.

3) A troop of cowards were 'decimated' – which meant having one soldier in every ten killed. The survivors were sent back into battle. Emperor Augustus made the nine 'lucky' soldiers club their 'unlucky' friend to death.

DID YOU KNOW…?

Roman army doctors didn't know about anaesthetics (to put you to sleep while they hacked you about!). They were trained not to hear your screams when they treated you.

ROTTEN ROMAN PUNISHMENT

The Romans were famous for making laws. It is said that Roman law was the start of most laws we still have today. But that doesn't mean the Roman laws were fair or free of cruelty. They weren't! If anyone tries to tell you the Romans had 'modern' laws, just remind them it was the Romans who liked to nail criminals to crosses.

In AD 64 there was a huge fire that destroyed a large area of Rome. The Romans were angry and looking for someone to blame. Emperor Nero accused a group of Jews who followed the teachings of Jesus: the Christians. He started executing them and the Romans enjoyed the idea. Add the stickers to read what the Roman historian, Tacitus, wrote…

History of Rome by Tacitus
Book 15, AD 62-65

Mockery of every sort was added to their deaths. They were covered with the skins of wild beasts, and then they were torn to death by ☐ or were nailed to ☐ or were thrown to the ☐ and burnt, to serve as flaming ☐ when darkness fell. Nero offered his gardens for the executions, and was putting on a show in the ☐ while he mixed with the people in the dress of a ☐ driver.

In the reign of Emperor Constantine (one of the 'kindest' emperors) there were over 60 crimes that could get you executed. He also invented a new type of execution … death by lead. Add the stickers to see how he did it. Don't try this at home. As you know, lead is poisonous. So watch out when you chew those pencils!

1) TIE THE VICTIM TO A POST

2) OPEN HIS MOUTH WIDE

3) POUR BOILING LEAD DOWN HIS THROAT!

Romans often tried to make a punishment
fit a crime. If you were a poacher who stole
someone else's deer, you may be sewn into
the skin of the deer then set free. After a
while hunting dogs would be sent after you.
They would think you were a deer (because
dogs are a bit stupid like that) and they
would tear you to pieces. Lead this
hungry dog through the Roman maze
to the criminal hiding in the centre.

DID YOU KNOW…?

The Romans used hooks on hated criminals because they believed they were 'unclean' – no one wanted to touch their dead bodies.

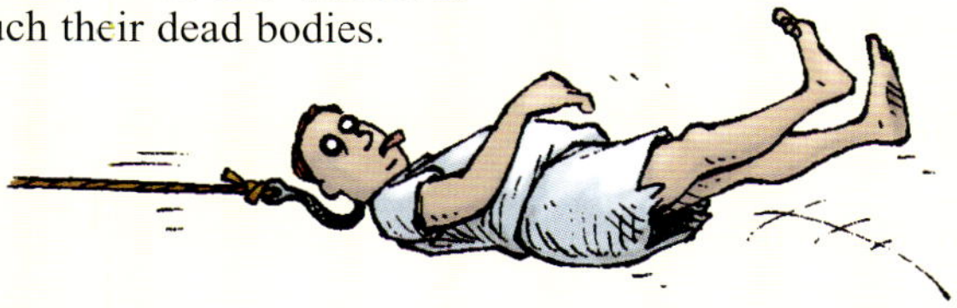

Can you add the correct stickers to match the punishment to the crime? It would be criminal if you got too many wrong. So, anyone who gets less than four out of six can punish themselves by writing 100 times: 'I am not verrey brite.'

1) STEALING CROPS

2) TELLING LIES ABOUT SOMEONE IN COURT

3) MURDERING YOUR WIFE BECAUSE SHE DRINKS WINE

4) SETTING FIRE TO YOUR NEIGHBOUR'S HOUSE (ARSON)

5) CALLING SOMEONE A NASTY NAME (SLANDER)

6) HAVING A BABY - IF YOU ARE A PRIESTESS

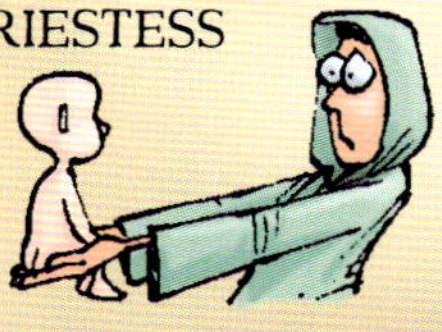

VICIOUS VIKING TIMES

The Vikings lived in Scandinavia – that's the posh word for Sweden, Denmark and Norway. The Saxons lived in England – they'd moved in when the Romans left. From AD 793, the Vikings started raiding Saxon England – and they weren't very nice about it! In fact, they were pretty vicious!

So why did the Vikings leave their homeland to cross the cold North Sea and raid England? Which of the following reasons have experts given for the Viking raids? Answer true or false and add the correct stickers.

VISIT THE SUNNY SAXON SHORES

1) It was getting too crowded in Scandinavia – the Vikings wanted more land.

2) They ran out of iron for their swords, spear heads and battle axes and needed a new supply.

3) The Vikings set off in their longboats to see if the world was round – on the way they bumped into England.

4) Viking rules meant that younger sons got no land when their fathers died – so they had to go overseas and pinch someone else's land.

5) There was a sudden shortage of herring in the North Sea – their main food supply – England had plenty of fish to share.

6) A change in climate made Scandinavia cold and uncomfortable – even wild, wet England was better than that.

7) Some pretty vicious kings took over in 9th-century Scandinavia – many Vikings sailed off to escape from them.

8) The Vikings needed more horns for their helmets and England had lots of bulls.

The Vikings were a tough lot in a violent age – and they were a hard bunch to get rid of. Match the stickers to the timeline to see how they raided and pillaged their way through Saxon England.

1) AD 787: Three boatloads of Vikings land on Dorset's coast. A Saxon tax officer orders them to appear before the Saxon king. The Vikings kill him.

2) AD 793: Comets, whirlwinds and dragons are seen over northern England. The first Viking attack on Lindisfarne Priory follows. Monks taken as slaves or thrown into the sea.

3) AD 871: Alfred becomes King of Wessex. He batters the Vikings at Eddington. He rules the south and lets the Viking Danes rule the north of England.

4) AD 1066: Viking Harald the Ruthless attacks York. English king Harold Godwinsson defeats him. But William of Normandy lands on the south coast of England. William defeats Harold. Normans rule – end of the Viking age.

Some people argue the Vikings were a loveable people who were very clever. It's true! They invented new ways for people to die. They lived in pretty vicious times. Add the stickers to match the following people to their sticky ends.

1) In AD 997 King Kenneth of Scotland wanted his son to be king after he died – other Scottish nobles didn't. So Kenneth was lured to a castle and taken to a room with a booby-trapped statue. When the statue was touched, several hidden crossbows were set off. The victim died in a hail of bolts.

2) King Edmund refused to fight the Vikings in AD 869. He wanted to convert them to Christianity. The Viking leader wanted to stick to the worship of Odin. King Edmund was tied to a tree and shot with arrows, then cut up and beheaded.

3) In AD 1012 the Archbishop of Canterbury was captured by the Vikings and a ransom of silver was asked for. The Archbishop refused to let his friends pay, so he was pelted with cattle bones and killed.

DID YOU KNOW?

Vikings loved their bloodthirsty weapons so much they even gave them names, such as "Adder" – because its bite could kill! What would you call yours?

VICIOUS VIKING INVADERS

The Vikings couldn't have carried out their raids on England – and Ireland – if they hadn't been great sailors and built superb boats. These boats had to be strong enough to cross the wild waves of the North Sea, yet still be slim enough to slip into the rivers that ran up to the rich Saxon towns.

The Viking ships are admired for their low, sleek look. But they weren't always like that. The story goes that one man bravely changed the shape of the Viking longboat. Add the stickers in the correct order to read this supposed true story...

ONE DAY A KING CAME TO INSPECT HIS NEW SHIP...

1	2	3
4	5	6

The Vikings had strict rules when sailing the seas. Read about what life was like on a longboat and match the correct picture stickers to the facts.

1) Vikings rarely took prisoners in sea battles because there was no room for them in the longboats. Instead they let the losers drown or killed them.

1

2) No one was allowed on board a longboat unless they had proved they were skilled with an oar, a sword and an axe.

2

3

3) Vikings knew which direction to sail, even in the middle of an uncharted ocean. They threw a raven into the air to see which way it flew to land.

4

4) When one Viking leader died a long way from home, his friends made monks boil his body till there were just bones, so they could carry them back in a box.

Imagine crossing the freezing North Sea in an open boat with no shelter or a hot water bottle. These conditions didn't worry the Vikings. They sailed even further – to Iceland, Greenland and even Newfoundland. Follow the routes from Scandinavia to find out who went where...

DID YOU KNOW?

The children's song, 'London Bridge is Falling Down', is about a Viking attack. English soldiers fired arrows from the bridge into the attacking longboats. So the Vikings attached ropes to the bridge's wooden legs and the other ends to the ships. They quickly rowed away. Result: London Bridge was falling down!

LIVE LIKE A VIKING

In Viking times, summers were short and wet, whilst in winter it snowed from October to February. Crops had little time to grow, and poor harvests meant no food. Vikings either went hunting or starved. Would you like to eat a stewed seagull or a polar bear steak? School dinners don't sound quite so bad now, do they?

Vikings ate cheese, smoked meats and bread. Food and soup was served in wooden bowls, and drink was poured into cups made from the horns of animals such as reindeer. Vikings used knives, fingers and sometimes very small spoons – but no forks. The picture below shows Viking food you wouldn't find in your local supermarket. Spot ten differences and circle them with a pencil.

DID YOU KNOW?

If you were a Viking in Iceland, and you wanted a bath, you'd pop down to the bath house. Water was poured over hot stones and you had a steam-clean. To really freshen up, you'd whip yourself with twigs … then run outside to roll in the snow.

Life wasn't easy for the women and children left behind while the men were doing a hard day's raiding. Add the stickers to read about Viking home life.

1) A WOMAN'S JOBS INCLUDED COMBING HUBBY'S ______ TO GET RID OF THE ______.

2) VIKING BOYS WOULD BEGIN TO ______ AS SOON AS THEY WERE OLD ENOUGH.

3) GIRLS WOULD BE ______ AND DOING ______ FOR MOST OF THEIR LIVES.

4) GIRLS ALSO LEARNED HOW TO ______ AND USE ______ IN CASE THEY WERE ATTACKED.

5) AS FOR LOO PAPER – IT WAS ______ OR NOTHING.

Life was horrible for the Viking slaves – the thralls. They had to work hard to make a living for no pay! Can you work out what jobs the boys did, and what jobs the girls did? Add the stickers to the correct panels.

JOBS FOR THE GIRLS

JOBS FOR THE BOYS

GRUESOME GODS AND SHOCKING SAGAS

Myths, sagas and tales of the supernatural were popular in Viking times. People believed that dwarves, giants and evil monsters were in constant battle. Story-tellers used to recite poems that told of disgusting deeds and horrible happenings. Gather round a blazing fire. It's story time – Viking style.

Christianity did not appeal to your average Viking – well, not until AD *960, but that's another story. The Vikings had lots of legends to believe in. Read the descriptions below and add the correct picture sticker.*

1) Loki, god of mischief. An evil character who caused lots of trouble amongst the other gods. Jealous, spiteful, cheeky. Sound like anyone you know?

2) Valhalla was a Viking heaven, where heroes went when they died. There, they fought all day and drank all night. If they were killed in heavenly battle, they came back to earth to fight the next day. During feasting, they drank from the skulls of their enemies.

3) Clouds are the brains of a dead giant. Or that's what they said in Viking days.

4) Thor, god of strength, hard work and storms. Vikings believed he made thunder by riding across the skies in his chariot. And he had a hammer which he liked A LOT.

5) The Vikings believed that the first man and woman came from the sweat of a giant's armpit.

DID YOU KNOW?

If you made a sacrifice to the gods and wanted all your neighbours to know how good you were, then you'd put it on poles outside your front door!

You may think the stories you heard as a child were vicious. Do you remember Jack and the Beanstalk, where the poor old giant bashes his brains on the ground? Vicious Viking legends are just as disgusting. Unscramble the words and add the correct word stickers to read this gruesome story...

LOKI WAS AN EVIL GOD WHO CAUSED [BLUEROT]. HE ONCE WAGERED HIS HEAD IN A BET WITH BROKK THE DWARF. LOKI LOST THE BET, BUT SAID BROKK COULDN'T TAKE HIS HEAD WITHOUT [GRHIMAN] HIS NECK! BROKK AND THE DWARVES GOT THEIR [GREENVE] BY [GESWIN] LOKI'S LIPS TOGETHER! THIS DID NOT STOP LOKI'S MISCHIEF-MAKING. HE GAVE HOD (THE SON OF CHIEF GOD, ODIN) A PIECE OF [TIMOLTEES]. HOD ATE THE MISTLETOE AND DIED. THE GODS DECIDED TO [PUSHIN] LOKI. THEY TIED HIM TO A TREE WITH HIS [TUGS] AND LEFT HIM THERE.

Viking poems gloried in death and destruction. Read this bloodthirsty ballad and find the words in CAPITAL LETTERS in the puzzle.
The words are written up, down, diagonally and across.

I have held a SWORD and SPEAR
When they were SLIPPERY with BLOOD.
HAWKS were hovering at the KILL,
As BRAVE the VIOLENT Vikings stood.

RED flames SWALLOWED up men's roofs
As we RAGED and CUT them down;
BODIES, SKEWERED, lay there sleepy
In the gateways of the town.

S	P	E	A	R	A	G	E	D
P	W	S	E	I	D	O	B	E
S	H	A	W	K	S	P	I	R
L	E	F	L	O	C	U	T	E
I	A	R	B	L	O	D	I	W
P	T	N	E	L	O	I	V	E
P	L	A	D	R	O	W	S	K
E	L	E	B	R	A	V	E	S
R	I	Q	O	E	N	T	I	D
Y	K	I	L	D	O	O	L	B

KING ALFRED THE GREAT

Just when it looked as if England was going to be overrun by the vicious Vikings, King Alfred the Great led the resistance in AD 871, and saved at least half of the country. Like many characters who lived in those days, the truth about Alfred's life is a bit mixed up with stories that told a few fibs to make him look like a great hero.

One such story tells of Alfred inventing the navy. He decided that it was a good idea to attack the Vikings at sea, before they landed. At sea, the Vikings were cramped into their longboats and couldn't fight and row at the same time. Work out which of the numbered squares are not part of the battle scene below.

DID YOU KNOW?

Some of Alfred's punishments were quite reasonable … but the Vikings quickly learned that he could be harsh on sea-raiders. In AD 896, Alfred's navy captured a lot of Viking raiders. They were taken to Winchester and hanged as pirates. Alfred had no more trouble with Viking raids after that!

King Alfred made a book of laws for the Saxons. For example, he worked out four ways of finding out if a person was guilty of a crime. They were called ordeals. If you passed through the ordeal, you were innocent. But if you failed, you suffered from both the test and then a punishment. Which would you choose? Match the stickers to each ordeal.

1) Ordeal by cake: A special cake is baked. Swear, "If I did this crime then may this cake choke me!" and eat the cake. If you're guilty, then you choke on the cake – if you're innocent, you live.

1

2) Ordeal by hot water: Put your arm into a pot of hot water and pull out a stone. Your arm will be bandaged for three days. After that, if your arm is healed, then you are innocent. But if there is a scald, then you are guilty and punished.

2

3) Ordeal by hot metal: Hold a rod of hot iron and walk with it for a set distance. Then, your hand is bandaged for three days. After that, if it's healed, you're innocent – if there's a burn on your hand, you're guilty.

3

4) Ordeal by cold water: You are tied hand and foot. A rope is placed around you and you are lowered into a pool. If you sink, then you are innocent. If you float, then you are guilty. You'll be dragged out and punished.

4

If you didn't like Alfred's Law, you could move to Danish England. Their rules were also brutal. If a man was beaten, and wanted his life spared, then he had to go through a harsh test. Add the stickers in the correct order to find out how to finish a Viking fight.

1) Play music on a fiddle and a drum.

2

3

5

6

4) The tail of the cow is covered with grease.

7) If you can hang on to the cow whilst it charges about the hall your life is spared.

THE AWFUL AZTECS

The Aztecs were Central American Indians. In the early 1300s, they arrived in the area we call Mexico today. The Aztecs were fierce and fearless fighters. They were also the neighbours from Hell. Within a few hundred years, they had made themselves the top tribe.

When the wandering Aztecs first arrived in Mexico, they were forced to become slaves for the people of Culhuacan. But even as slaves, the Aztecs were a nuisance. The Lord of Culhuacan was the man in charge. He sent the Aztecs off to fight a powerful enemy who would finish them off … at least that's what he thought. Match the picture stickers to the correct statements to see how the Aztecs survived and began their rise to power.

1) Victorious Aztec warriors returned from battle with mountains of their defeated enemy's ears, and presented them to the Lord of Culhuacan.

1

2) The Aztecs had proved they were great warriors. They requested a princess from a Mexican tribe called the Toltecs so that they could have some noble blood in their families.

2

3) The Aztecs took away the princess. She was sacrificed to become the Aztecs' goddess of war. The Toltec lord was so cross with the Aztecs that he drove them out of his land.

3

4) The Aztecs believed that the sun was a god who had power over human life. To keep this god happy, the Aztecs fed it with a regular supply of human hearts.

4

5) Fortunately, the Aztecs preferred sacrificing their enemies! They brutally fought neighbouring tribes, took their land and food and sacrificed the captives to the sun god.

5

6) The Aztecs came to settle in Teotihuacan, a rich land where the great pyramids were. They had a strong base from which to fight their enemies. The Aztecs had begun their rise to power.

6

The city of Teotihuacan was massive and the twin pyramids of the Great Temple looked down on the streets. These streets were kept clean by thousands of sweepers every day. The sweepers were usually captives from other tribes who were forced to serve the Aztecs. Add the missing word stickers from this young sweeper's diary.

14 DECEMBER

It's wet, cold and _____ work on the streets. At least it's a quiet time for the _____ None of the _____ bits to sweep up!

26 JANUARY

Today's the day they grab the _____ and pull them by the _____ to make them _____ Mum used to do it to me – I'm tall – I've a neck like a _____

28 JANUARY

Today, children have their ears _____. I held my little brother down while our mum _____ the holes – he didn't _____

16 MARCH

The young warriors have mock _____. The priests make the usual sacrifices and wear the _____ of the _____. My friend cleans at the temple and says they smell _____ !

Life wasn't as hard for the emperor. Although, he did have to tell someone what a feeble little human being he was, and then spend four days fasting. The words in CAPITALS below need to go into the grid. The number in brackets tells you where the words fit. The blue column will tell you who the emperor spoke to.

LIVE LIKE AN AZTEC

The Aztec child was taught not to expect a happy life … and it didn't get one! Boys were trained to be warriors and told, 'Your mission is to give the sun the blood of your enemies to drink.' Girls, on the other hand, were told their place was in the home!

If you wanted the gods to bring you rain or a good harvest, then you had to give them a gift, a really precious gift, like the life of a child. The Aztecs must have really loved children because they sacrificed dozens every year! Add the picture stickers to complete these other chilling facts about the not-so-great Aztec childhood.

1) A disobedient child would be pinched on the arms or the [ ] .

2) Extremely wicked children would be held over a [ ] of roasting chilli-peppers to breathe in the stinging [ ] .

3) Some really evil children have been [ ] up and left to die in the cold and mud.

4) Pottery figures show Mexican boys grinning with their top [ ] filed to a point!

5) If a child died, it would be buried in a [ ] .

So you survive an Aztec childhood. Maybe you fought a few battles along the way. But what happens when you die? Well, the Aztec custom is for your body to be buried under your house! Find the path to the dead body – before the rats get it!

If you were an Aztec boy who wanted to marry the girl of his dreams, there were various things that had to be done, and in a specific order. Would you have made a good Aztec? See if you can stick the correct stickers in the blank spaces.

1) FIRST CHOOSE YOUR BRIDE. WHO GETS YOU PERMISSION TO MARRY THE GIRL?

1

2) WHO DO YOU ASK?

2

3) YOU ALSO NEED PERMISSION TO GET MARRIED YOURSELF. WHO DO YOU ASK?

3

4) HOW DO YOU CHOOSE YOUR WEDDING DAY?

4

5) THE WEDDING TAKES PLACE AFTER A FEAST. HOW DOES THE BRIDE GET TO YOUR HOUSE FOR THE CEREMONY?

5

6) HOW DO THE GUESTS GET FROM THE FEAST TO THE WEDDING AT YOUR HOUSE?

6

7) EVERYONE GIVES YOU A WEDDING PRESENT. WHEN DO YOU GET YOUR GIFTS?

7

8) HOW ARE YOU JOINED TOGETHER IN MARRIAGE?

8

9) THERE IS A FINAL FEAST WITH ALCOHOL TO DRINK. BUT ONLY CERTAIN PEOPLE ARE ALLOWED TO DRINK. WHO?

9

DID YOU KNOW...?

There was a quick and easy way for poor families to make some money. Sell their kids! Slave traders would buy healthy children and take them to market to sell on.

FUNNY FOOD AND GORY GAMES

But life wasn't all work and no play. The Aztecs ate well (even if some of it was human flesh), got drunk and even played a ball game that they'd picked up from the Maya – an ancient Mexican tribe.

Thanks to the Aztecs, we have chilli pepper for curries, corn for cornflakes and tomatoes for the sauce in baked beans. There are some things they used to eat that you may not be so keen to taste. Find the not-so-tasty treats in the wordsearch. The words can be found written forwards, backwards, up, down, diagonally and across.

MONKEYS, TOADS, FROGS, CACTUS, DOGS, TADPOLES, ANTS, LARVAE, LIZARDS

T	A	D	P	O	L	E	S	T
M	E	N	L	I	A	R	G	Y
S	G	O	R	F	R	D	O	S
Y	O	I	E	D	V	G	D	F
E	G	S	D	R	A	Z	I	L
K	L	D	U	O	E	R	M	H
N	C	A	C	T	U	S	O	T
O	M	O	H	I	F	E	D	S
M	R	T	E	G	S	T	N	A

So that's the food taken care of, but what did the Aztecs drink? Unjumble the letters and add the correct word stickers to find out how to make a top Aztec teatime treat – honey beer.

1) ALCOHOL WAS MADE FROM THE RUNNY [HEY NO] OF BEES.

2) THE HONEY NEEDED [A BEAR TIC] (GERMS) TO TURN IT INTO ALCOHOL.

3) GIRLS TOOK THE HONEY INTO THEIR [HOT SUM], SWISHED IT ROUND AND THEN [TAPS] IT OUT INTO A LARGE BOWL.

4) AFTER A FEW DAYS, THE CONTENTS OF THE [BLOW] BEGAN TO [FORTH] AND [BE BULB] AND SLOWLY TURN INTO ALCOHOL.

DON'T TRY THIS AT HOME – ALL THAT HONEY-SWISHING WILL MAKE YOUR [THE ET] ROT!

The Aztecs enjoyed playing a jolly little game called pok-a-tok. The idea was that the better you played the 'ball game', the happier the gods would be, and the better the crops would grow. You scored by putting a ball through a ring by using your arms and legs. Oh, and the game was played to the death. Spot ten differences between the two pictures below and circle them with a pencil.

DID YOU KNOW...?

Aztecs ate larvae, which are insects before they grow up. So fly larvae (known as maggots) and beetle larvae (known as grubs) were both on the menu!

SCARY SACRIFICES

The Aztecs wanted to keep their sun god happy. An angry sun god could make them suffer – scorching their land or sending a plague of locusts to eat the crops. Some people think their god will be happy with a bit of praise and a few hymns. The awful Aztecs believed you had to give human lives to their god – thousands of them. And not only that, they had to be sacrificed in a gruesomely gory way!

Health warning: if you are sickened at the sight of a squashed rabbit on the road, do NOT attempt this activity. On the other hand, if you like a bit of gore, then see if you can find the five missing stickers to put these six stages of sacrifice in the correct order.

The Aztecs' favourite sacrifices were enemy warriors. The braver the enemy, the better the sacrifice. There were five main ways of sacrificing victims – some more cruel than others. See if you can match the correct picture sticker to the method of sacrifice.

1) Lie the victim on their back over the sacrificial stone, open the chest with a knife, pull out the heart and offer it to the gods.

1

2

2) Cut off the head. Girls would sometimes go to the temple and had to pretend to be a god. The head chop was their payment!

3) Tie the victim to a large rock and give him a sword club to defend himself. He then fights against an Aztec warrior whose sword club has a knife edge.

3

4

4) Tie the victim to poles. Mark his heart with a white spot, and fill him full of darts or arrows. Don't aim at that spot with the first few arrows.

5) Throw the victim into a fire then pull him out, repeat a few times. When he's lightly baked, do the heart sacrifice.

5

Some victims were sacrificed in front of a statue of the goddess Coatlicue. She had a double head and a necklace of hearts, skulls and severed hands. Work out which of the numbered pictures below are part of the image.

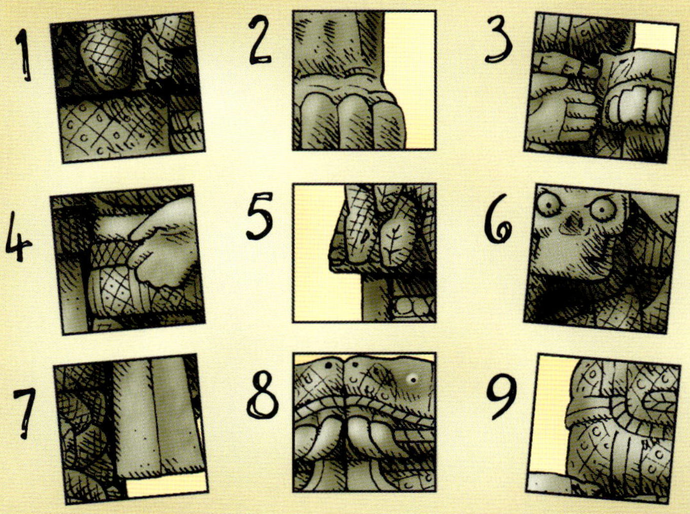

THE CUNNING CONQUISTADORS

Aztec men lived to fight. When the war drum sounded, every Aztec man picked up his weapons and joined his group of 800 men. But no amount of bravery could beat the cunning Spanish conquistadors. With the use of guns – and with a lot of luck – they defeated even the bravest Aztec warriors and seized control of the Aztec empire.

See what fantastic facts you know about the Aztec warriors by trying this quirky quiz. Answer TRUE or FALSE and add the correct stickers.

1) Young Aztec men could be made full warriors by having their faces smeared with the blood of a cow's leg.

2) The Aztecs had wooden clubs, edged with stone blades that were powerful enough to cut off a horse's head.

3) Aztec leaders were easy to spot because they wore large feather and reed constructions on their shoulders.

4) Warriors believed that dying in battle was a terrible thing.

5) Rich Aztec warriors wore gold and jewels when they went into battle.

6) Warriors didn't get their hair cut till they'd killed someone in battle.

7) Warriors short of food would eat their dead friends.

8) Aztecs believed in killing themselves rather than being captured.

9) Aztec warriors wore shiny metal armour.

10) The Aztec army needed to capture 20 enemy fighters for sacrifice and no less.

11) Aztecs believed that precious stones held magical powers.

12) Aztec warriors believed that if they died in battle they would turn into monkeys.

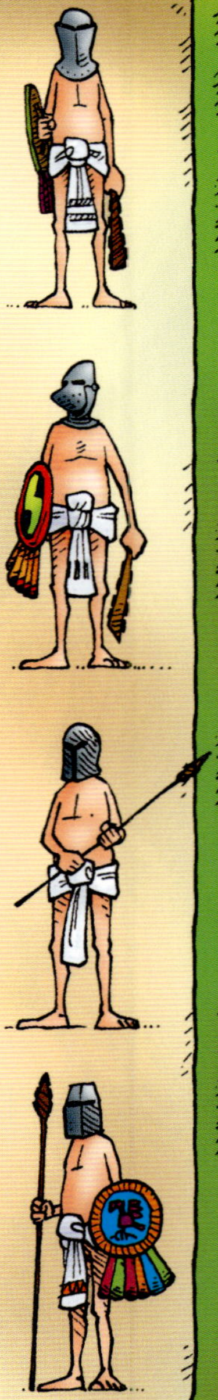

ROTTEN ROMAN STICKERS

Stickers for ROTTEN ROMAN RULERS

TRUE

FALSE

TRUE

FALSE

TRUE

FALSE

WIFE

CORPSE

SMASH

DROWN

HORSE.

CHICKEN

EATING

COBWEB

MOTHER.

RULE

CHEESE.

RIVER TIBER

LEG

Stickers for ROTTEN ROMAN PUNISHMENTS

A. NO PUNISHMENT

D. THROWN OFF THE TARPEIAN ROCK

F. EXECUTED BY BEING STRANGLED IN PRISON

E. BURNED ALIVE

B. WALLED UP ALIVE

C. CLUBBED TO DEATH

Stickers for GRUESOME GAMES

Stickers for FEARSOME FIGHTE

FIGHTERS

SPORT

DEFEATED.

WRONG

MURDERERS.

ESCAPE

BODIES

VICIOUS VIKING STICKERS

Stickers for VICIOUS VIKING INVADERS

Stickers for LIVE LIKE A VIKING

FARMING

HOUSEWORK

HAIR -

NITS

RAID

WEPONS

MOSS

SWIM

SPREAD MANURE

GRIND CORN BY HAND

MILK COWS AND GOATS

MAKE CHEESE

BUILD WALLS

WASH

COOK

Stickers for KING ALFRED THE GREAT

Stickers for VICIOUS VIKING INVADERS

ANGRY AZTEC STICKERS

Stickers for LIVE LIKE AN AZTEC

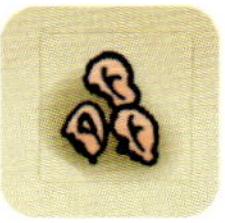

nasty

skins

muddy

battles

neck

victims

FALSE

FALSE

FALSE

FALSE

FALSE

TRUE

FALSE

TRUE

Stickers for CUNNING CONQUISTADORS

Stickers for FUNNY FOOD AND GORY GAMES

BACTERIA

BUBBLE

MOUTHS

TEETH

FROTH

HONEY

BOWL

SPAT

sacrifices

rattlesnake!

drilled

grow

dreadful

children

pierced

squawk

TRUE

TRUE

TRUE

TRUE

Stickers for SCARY SACRIFICES

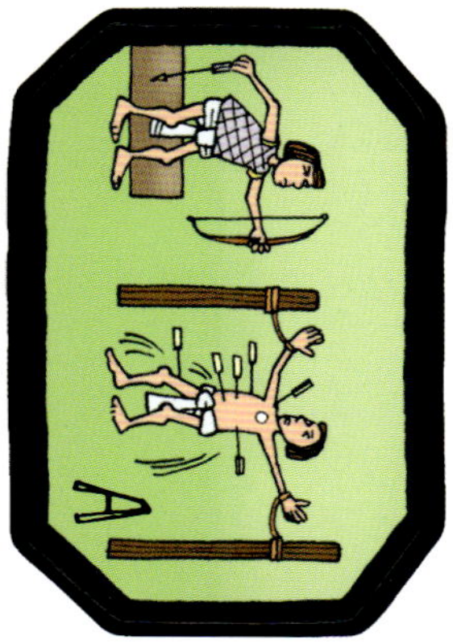

SPARE STICKERS

Stickers for THE AWFUL AZTECS

Stickers for LIVE LIKE A VIKING

DIG PEAT FOR FUEL

HERD PIGS AND GOATS

SPARE STICKERS

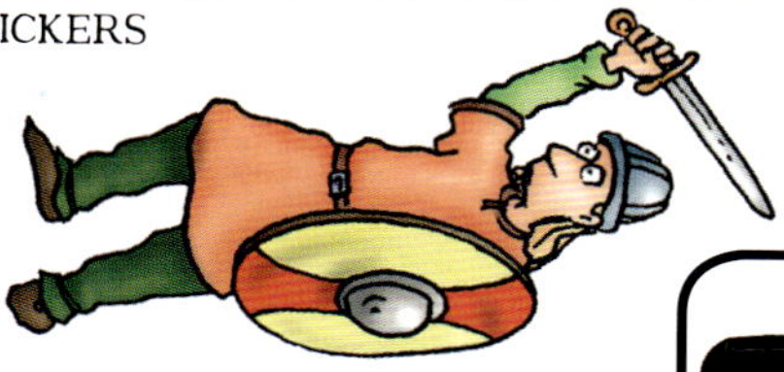

Stickers for GRUESOME GODS AND SHOCKING SAGAS

Stickers for VICIOUS VIKING INVADERS

MISTLETOE

PUNISH

SEWING

TROUBLE

HARMING

REVENGE

GUTS

TRUE

FALSE

FALSE

TRUE

TRUE

TRUE

TRUE

FALSE

Stickers for VICIOUS VIKING TIMES

Stickers for FEARSOME FIGHTERS

SPARE STICKERS

Stickers for ROTTEN ROMAN ARMY

Stickers for ROTTEN ROMAN PUNISHMENTS

DARK KNIGHTS AND DINGY CASTLES STICKERS

Stickers for DARK KNIGHTS

FALSE

FALSE

FALSE

FALSE

FALSE

TRUE

TRUE

TRUE

TRUE

TRUE

THE BOOT

THE RACK

THUMBSCREWS

THE GAUNTLETS

SKEFFINGTON'S GYVES

Stickers for CRAZY CASTLE LIFE

Stickers for KNIGHTLY ORDERS

TERRIBLE TUDOR STICKERS

Stickers for WHAT IS A TERRIBLE TUDOR

YEA

YEA NAY

YEA YEA

NAY NAY

Stickers for HORRIBLE HENRY VIII

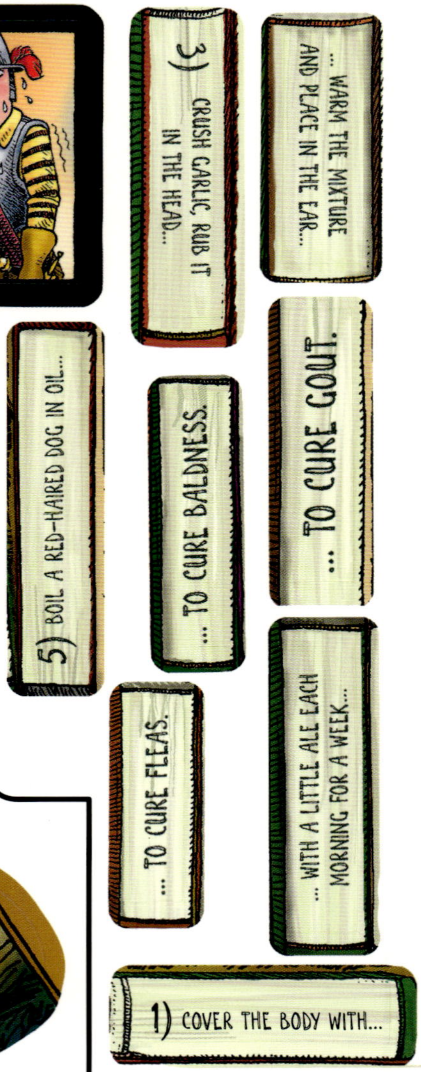

Stickers for TERRIBLE TUDOR LIFE & DEATH

Stickers for SLIMY STUART TIMES

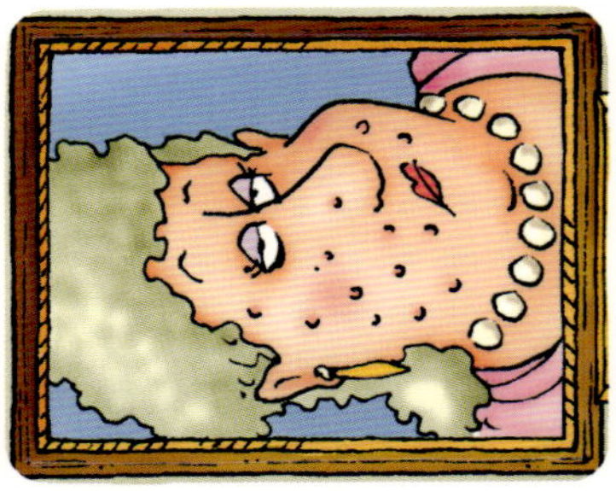

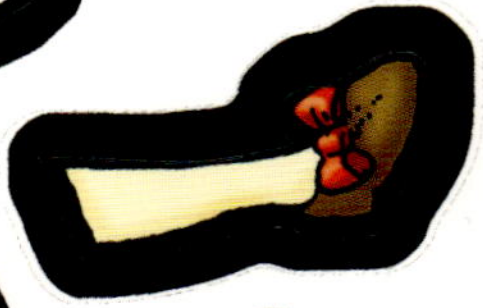

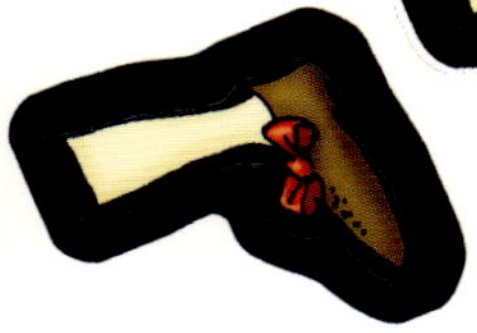

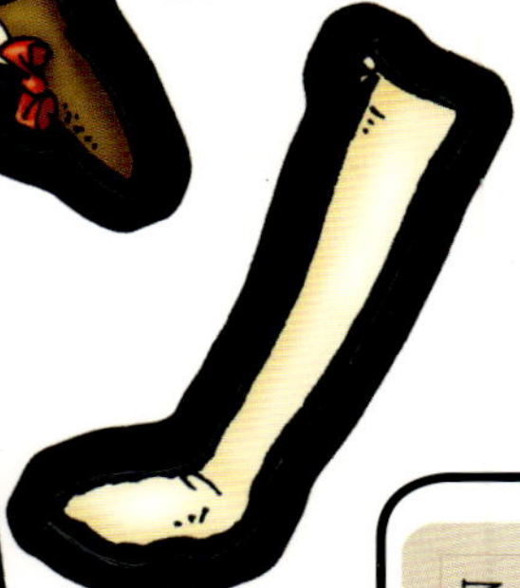

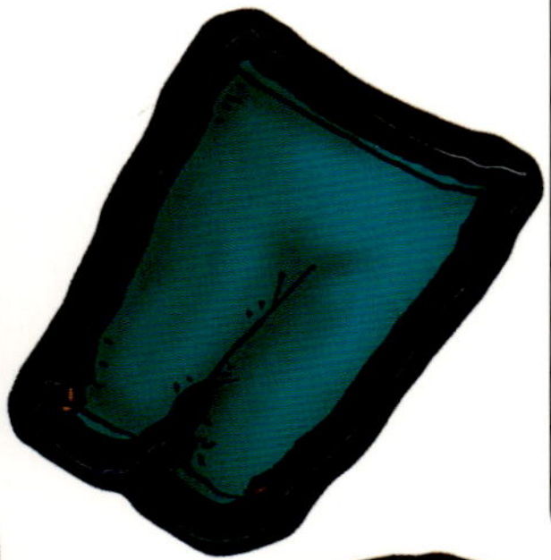

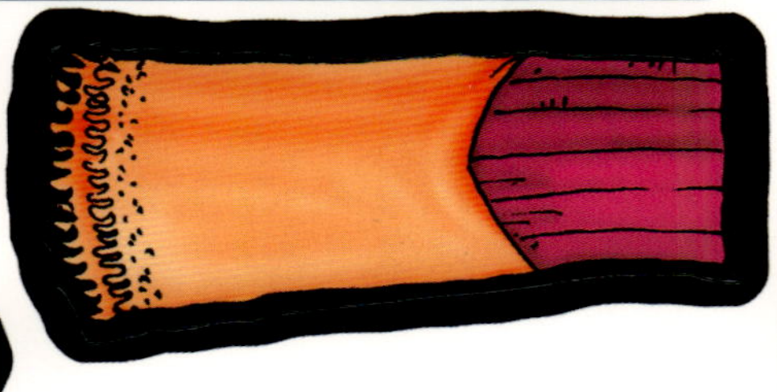

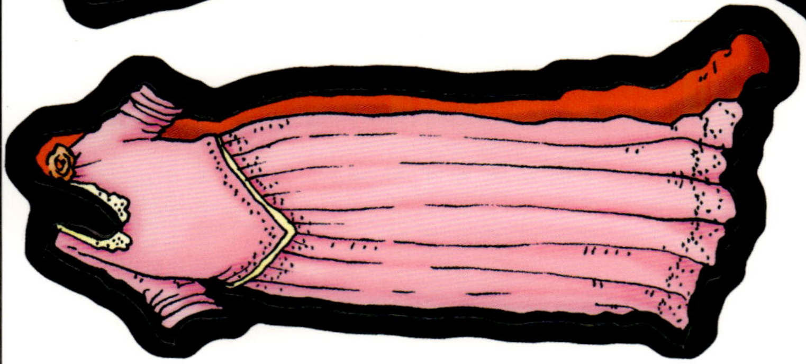

FIRE

WOODEN

SMOKE

CHARLES

PEOPLE

LOAF

STREET

Stickers for STUART CHILDREN

SLIMY STUART STICKERS

Stickers for CRIME AND PAINFUL PUNISHMENT

ASHES

KING

BAKER

BURNING

Stickers for DEADLY STUART DAYS

Stickers for TUDOR CRIME & TERRIBLE PUNISHMENT

head

foaming

boiling

squeezes

toads

survive

tongues

'toad-eater'

poison

Stickers for STRANGE STUART FADS

TRUE

TRUE

FALSE

TRUE

FALSE

TRUE

TRUE

TRUE

FALSE

FALSE

bodies,

dead.

cut

fire,

prison

hanged

bowels

execution

Stickers for STUART CHILDREN

Stickers for CRUEL CRUSADES

ORGANS

NAVELS

ENTRAILS

DEATH.

DRAG

KILL

BARE

FLOG

ATTACK

SHOOT

CUT

Stickers for SCARY SACRIFICES

Stickers for CRAZY CASTLE LIFE

SPARE STICKERS

Aztec warriors were led by an emperor called Motecuhzoma who believed in superstitions and 'signs' that only his magicians could explain. See how good a magician you are by finding the stickers that 'explain' these five signs.

1

2

3

4

5

DID YOU KNOW...?

Aztec warriors believed a finger and some hair from a woman who had died giving birth would protect them when they went to war. And they were prepared to dig up a body to get their hands on a magic finger!

The invading Spanish were shocked to discover a 'skull rack' near the temple at Teotihuacan. Hundreds of skulls were set in cement and poles stood on top. Count up the number of skulls in each of the three columns. Add these numbers together and multiply by 1,000 to discover how many skulls the Spanish counted.

DARK KNIGHTS

Knights were soldiers who fought on horseback from around AD 1000 to about 1600. They were dangerous men. Men who said they'd be true to their leader (some hope), polite to everyone (fat chance) and defend the weak (you must be joking).

1) About AD 500 China
The stirrup is invented. Now warriors can fight on horseback without falling off the saddle.

1

2) About AD 1000 France
Norman horsemen stop throwing their spears and start using them underarm to stab. The lance is born. The clever Normans invent chainmail at around the same time.

2

3) Early 1100s
'Tournaments' turn war into a sport.

3

4) Late 1100s
Poems about knights become popular in France. Tournaments become respectable.

4

5) 1300s
A scoring system to decide the winner in a friendly combat is created.

5

6) 1320s
The cannon is first used in battle. Feeble thing. No one worries too much about them … yet!

6

7) 1327
Knights are wearing complete suits of 'plate' armour instead of chainmail. (No, not dinner plates, stupid.)

7

8) 1346 France
At the Battle of Crécy, English archers stuff French knights. The power of the knight in battle is disappearing.

8

9) 1464
Mighty Bamburgh Castle on the Scottish border is captured using just two cannons. The power of the castle is disappearing.

9

10) 1621
Last of the old tournaments in England.

10

Knights had more rules than your school. It's true they didn't have daft ones like, 'Don't run in the corridor,' or 'Don't let the tyres down on the head teacher's car.' But they did have rules ... some of which you could still follow today. Unscramble the words to find out about them.

KNIGHTLY RULES

- Spend your ONE MY wisely
- Choose NERDS IF carefully
- Go to church NET OF
- Always be A DYER for TABLET
- Be A VERB in battle
- Don't go THUG INN too often
- If you are IDLE NUTS seek revenge

D	O	N	E	I	D	E	S
T	R	I	P	O	L	I	S
L	O	V	E	R	R	E	E
R	U	D	E	L	O	C	T
L	N	A	M	O	W	A	N
O	S	M	E	O	P	F	U
V	E	R	F	U	A	J	O
E	D	E	L	T	S	A	C

But, above all else, a knight should be a lover. A knight without a woman-friend was like a bun without a beefburger! He was empty. A woman-friend was someone who gave his life a real purpose. Jaufre RUDEL was often seen as the perfect example of a knightly LOVER. Jaufre was in LOVE with the great Countess of TRIPOLI. She was said to be ONE of the most beautiful women in the WORLD. Even though JAUFRE had never seen the WOMAN, this didn't stop him from sending her endless love POEMS. At last, the COUNTESS invited Jaufre to meet her. He walked into her CASTLE, took one look at her beautiful FACE and ... what? Find the words in CAPITALS in the wordsearch. They are written forwards, backwards, up, down and across. The remaining letters will tell you what happened to Jaufre.

Jaufre _ _ _ _ _ on the spot

DID YOU KNOW...?

Henry V was a great believer in chivalry. He believed a knight should not be killed if it could be helped. And a knight should never be killed by a peasant. Henry's favourite groom was a peasant. At a siege in Montereau the groom accidentally killed a knight. Henry had the peasant hung.

KNIGHTLY ORDERS

Rule one of chivalry was, 'Fight no matter how hopeless the battle!' But, before a person could become a fighting knight, they had to start as a page with long boring hours of practice. Then, if they had proved themselves, they became a squire, and then finally they could join a special knight's club – an Order.

Imagine you're a boy back in medieval days – how do you become a knight? You will need a dice and a playing partner. Take turns rolling the dice and move on the number of spaces shown – use pennies as counters. If you land on a joust, go up. If you land on a sword, go down. The first to reach the end can have a good night out, good knight!

These days only the monarch of the United Kingdom can make someone a knight in a very special club – a Knight of the 'Order of the Garter'. In the Middle Ages, a garter was a piece of ribbon women tied round their legs to keep their stockings up. In 1347, King Edward III wanted to create an Order of the Round Table. Then something happened to change his mind. Add the stickers in the correct order to find out what.

If the Queen won't make you one of her 25 Knights of the Garter then you could always make up your own Order and knight your friends! To give you an idea, here are some Orders from Europe – the Order of the Elephant, the Order of the Thistle, the Order of the Bath and the Order of the Golden Fleece. Colour in the dotted areas to see if you can work out which Order the knight in the picture is from.

1

2

3

4

5

6

7

DID YOU KNOW...?

Some squires from poor families could not afford to buy their weapons and become knights. They stayed squires all of their lives!

TERRIFIC TOURNAMENTS

Some knights were desperate for a fight, so desperate they went out looking for them. They stood at crossroads and challenged passing horsemen to friendly battles. Then, in the early 1060s, a French knight called Geoffrey de Preuilly organized these challenges into 'tournaments' and knights began to use the tournaments as a way in which they could practise their skills.

Tournaments took war and turned it into a game. But the aim was still to capture an opposing knight and hold him to ransom. There were no referees or judges at first, but there were 'safe areas' where a battered knight would be allowed to escape and rest. What do you imagine the rules were? Tick the rules you would agree with. Turn to the answer page to see if you would have made a good knight.

1) Do not gang up in a group to attack another knight.
2) Do not attack a knight who has lost some armour.
3) Do not use bows, arrows or cross bows.
4) Do not hide and ambush opponents.
5) Do not touch a knight in a safe area.
6) Do not attack a knight who has lost his horse.
7) Do not attack a knight from behind.
8) Do not attack a knight waving a white flag.
9) Do not strike below the belt with the sword.
10) Do not kill another knight.

Tournaments were all about winning prizes. If you go to a fairground today you could throw darts or fire air rifles to win a cuddly panda or a china dog. Prizes in medieval times included velvet caps, bears, silver lions and talking parrots. Can you work out what each of the knights A, B, C and D have won?

As well as tournaments there were jousts. A man in a can with a lance trying to knock another man in a can off his horse. Spot ten differences between the two pictures below and circle them with a pencil.

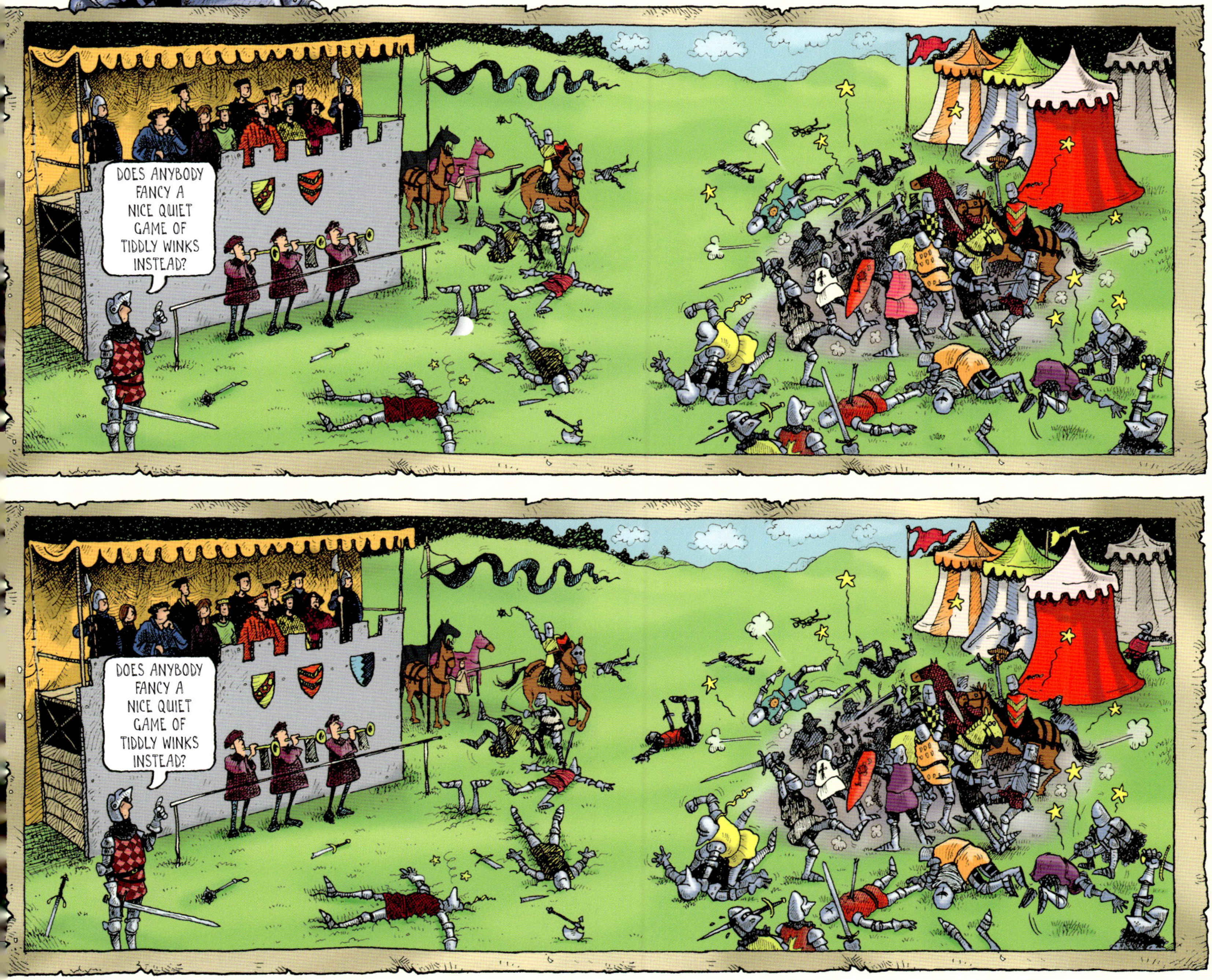

DID YOU KNOW...?

A knight could have an assistant, his squire, carry fresh weapons to him in the jousting area. But the squires sometimes got carried away and started using the weapons on the opposing squires. A new rule was invented. It said that any squire carrying a sword into the fighting area had to hold it by the point! Ouch!

CRUEL CRUSADES

Early Christians believed that war was evil and Christians shouldn't fight, until AD 590 when Pope Gregory said that non-Christians had to be converted to Christianity, by whatever means – threats, war, death! So when knights came along 500 years after Pope Greg, they had the perfect excuse for fighting – a war against enemies of the Christian religion, known as a Crusade.

In 1095, Pope Urban II decided it was time the Christians took over Jerusalem. It was their Holy City, but it was full of Turks, who were Muslims. The Muslims weren't going to give the city up without a fight. The Pope needed men with swords to drive the Turks out. Add the missing stickers to find out what the Pope said in order to get knights to fight for him.

Of course, the Pope didn't know what he was talking about. He was repeating stories that he'd heard. But it worked and the first of many Crusades to the Middle East began. In 1095, when the First Crusade set off, one group of pilgrims found a goose that they thought was sent by God. They began to play Follow My Leader with it. When they ran out of food they probably played Eat My Leader! Can you lead the group of pilgrims to the goose?

THE TURKS CUT OPEN THE ____ OF CHRISTIANS THAT THEY WANT TO TORMENT WITH A LOATHSOME ____ THEY TEAR OUT THEIR ____ AND TIE THEM TO A STAKE. THEY ____ THEIR VICTIMS ROUND THE STAKE AND ____ THEM. THEY ____ THEM AS THEY LIE FLAT ON THE GROUND WITH THEIR ____ OUT. THEY TIE SOME TO POSTS AND ____ THEM FULL OF ARROWS. THEY ORDER OTHERS TO ____ THEIR NECKS AND ____ THEM WITH SWORDS TRYING TO SEE IF THEY CAN ____ OFF THEIR HEADS WITH A SINGLE STROKE.

The stories the Pope said were mostly lies and the Turks were no worse than the Christians. In fact, the Christian soldiers went on to be a lot worse! Which of the following statements about the First Crusade are true and which are false? Add the correct word stickers.

1) The people who chose to fight the Muslims cut out red crosses and sewed them on their tunics.

2) People who went on the Crusades were told if they were killed they would go to Heaven.

3) Crusaders didn't have to pay tax.

4) A priest called Peter the Panda led a Crusade consisting mainly of peasants.

5) The Crusaders ran out of fresh water and ended up drinking their own urine.

6) Food was plentiful – no one went hungry.

7) When the Crusaders captured the town of Maarart, they boiled the Turks in cooking pots and ate them.

8) The Crusaders finally reached Jerusalem and climbed over the high city walls on 25 December, 1097.

9) The Turks hid gold in their shoes to stop the Crusaders from having it.

10) The Crusade was a success – Jerusalem was captured. Pope Urban II led a victory parade in Rome.

DID YOU KNOW...?

In 1119 Crusader Count Robert was captured in battle and taken before the Atabeg of Damascus. The Atabeg drew his sword and cut off Robert's head. As if that wasn't cruel enough he threw Robert's body to the dogs but kept his skull. It was encrusted with jewels and used as a drinking cup.

CRAZY CASTLE LIFE

Knights had to have something solid to live in – and a home they thought would be safe. A bungalow in Brighton wasn't good enough for a knight, oh no. He had to build a posh stone pile with creepy corridors, twisting turrets and dingy dungeons. A knight's home was definitely his castle!

Most castles had a dreadful dungeon – an underground place where prisoners could be tortured – a sort of playroom from Hell. Instead of toys, they were filled with instruments of torture. Can you add the correct names to see what some of the torture equipment was called?

1

1) The prisoner stood on blocks of wood. His or her wrists were fastened in handcuffs to a beam above the head. One by one the blocks were removed till the prisoner finally was swinging from the beam.

2

2) A piece of heavy wood was placed down each side of the prisoner's legs. Wedges were hammered in between the leg and the wood so that the leg was steadily crushed.

3

3) The victim was laid on a wooden frame and ropes tied his or her hands and feet to a roller at each end. As the rollers were turned in opposite directions, the prisoner was stretched.

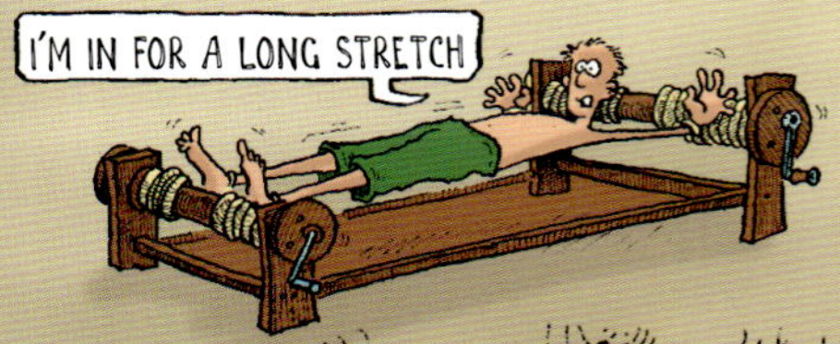

4

4) This was an iron hoop in two halves joined by a hinge. The prisoner, hands tied behind, knelt in one half while the torturer closed the second half shut. The prisoner was squeezed into a tight ball.

5

5) The victim's thumbs were placed under a metal bar. The bar was slowly screwed down so that it squeezed the fingernails.

In 1066, when William the Conqueror invaded England, he and his Norman conquerors started to build castles with wooden walls and towers. In the early 1100s, castles were made more solid and were built from stone like Cutter Whey Castle, which is two miles to the west of Blackpool … at least it was. Can you work out which of the numbered squares are part of the scene below?

1  2  3 

4  5  6 

Castles were really fun places to live in. They didn't have the boring things that we have today … but it has to be said, they were pretty dingy. Read about some of the things knights had to do without and add the correct stickers.

1) *Double glazing*. Instead they had draughts. Shutters were put over the window spaces to keep out the cold, but they didn't stop the draughts.

1

2

2) *Toilets*. They just had garderobes – little rooms that jutted out from the castle walls. Human waste dropped straight down into the moat below.

3) *Electric cookers*. They just had wood-burning ovens and open fires. Meat would turn on a spit. The meat would be a bit burned on the outside and a bit raw on the inside.

3

4

4) *Carpets*. They just had reeds that were scattered on the floor to mop up the grease spilled.

5) *Beds*. Except for his lordship's. Peasants like you would just sleep on the floor.

5

WHAT IS A TERRIBLE TUDOR?

The Tudors were a family who ruled England, and poked their noses into the rest of Great Britain, from 1485 till 1603. Henry VII was the grandfather, his son was Henry VIII and Edward VI, Mary I and Elizabeth I were the grandchildren. Five rulers and 118 years that changed the lives of the English people. Some members of this family were truly terrifying tyrants – even worse than teachers!

Confused by which monarch is which? Match the portrait stickers to the correct limericks to create your very own 'Tudor Hall of Fame'.

Henry Tudor beat Richard the Thirder
When the battle turned into pure murder.
Henry pinched Richard's crown
For the ride back to town.
He was top man! He could go no furder.

King Henry was fat as a boar
He had six wives and still wanted more.
Anne and Kate said,
"By heck! He's a pain in the neck!"
As their heads landed smack on the floor.

At nine years the little King Eddie
Had a grip on the throne quite unsteady.
He was all skin and bone,
Grown men fought for his throne
And by sixteen young Eddie was deadie.

Bloody Mary, they say, was quite mad.
And the nastiest taste that she had
Was for protestant burning –
Seems she had a yearning
To kill even more than her dad.

A truly great queen was old Lizzie,
She went charging around being busy.
She thought herself beaut,
But her teeth looked like soot
And her hair it was all red and frizzy.

Henry VIII was fat, ruthless and cruel. What more could you want in a monarch? Much of his time was spent having wives or Catholics killed. Read Henry's horrible timeline and match the cartoon stickers to the key events.

1

1) 1509: Henry VIII takes the throne because his older brother, Arthur, has carelessly died. Big Hen not only takes Arthur's crown but his wife, Catherine, too.

2

2) 1536: Henry decides he wants rid of his old wife Cathy – so he puts himself in charge of the Church and grants himself a divorce. The old Catholic Church and its monks and monasteries are banned.

3

3) 1536: Soon Henry starts chopping wives. He also divorces some of them. Favourite wife, Jane, dies giving birth to their son, Edward – who'll become next Tudor king.

4

4) 1547: Mad, bad Henry VIII dies (which saves a lot on the palace food bills). He leaves England poorer and divided, and sickly, nine-year-old Edward VI, in charge. Sad.

Being the wife of Henry VIII wasn't a bed of roses. Having a son was your job. If you failed, you lost your head. Or you were divorced. Or even after you had a son, you still died anyway. Add the stickers to show what happened to each wife and if they had any children.

CHILDREN
=GIRL =BOY
=NO CHILDREN

WHAT HAPPENED
=DIVORCED =DIED
=BEHEADED =SURVIVED

1) CATHERINE OF ARAGON
QUEEN – APR 1506 TO APR 1533

2) ANNE BOLEYN
QUEEN – JAN 1533 TO MAY 1536

3) JANE SEYMOUR
QUEEN – MAY 1536 TO OCT 1537

4) ANNE OF CLEVES
QUEEN – JAN 1540 TO JULY 1540

5) CATHERINE HOWARD
QUEEN – JULY 1540 TO FEB 1541

6) CATHERINE PARR
QUEEN – JULY 1543 TO JAN 1547

DID YOU KNOW...?

Old Henry was very 'kind' when it came to Anne Boleyn's execution. He didn't want any of that hacking about and sawing at necks. He sent for a real expert. A swordsman. With one swing, Anne's head was clean off!

HORRIBLE HENRY VIII

You know that Henry VIII had six wives. But did you know that Henry reigned for 38 torturing Tudor years and, in that time, about 72,000 people were executed? That's about 1,900 a year, or five every day. It must have been a bit like a National Lottery with 35 losers every week.

Henry wanted power over everything and everyone – this included the Church. So he got rid of the Catholic Church and made himself head of a Church of England. Henry killed or tortured anyone who opposed it. Here is a list of some of Henry's horrible laws. Work out which ones are TRUE or FALSE and add the correct stickers, YEA for yes, NAY for no.

TO THE PEOPLE OF ENGLAND

In the name of His Most Royal Majesty,
King Henry VIII, defender of the faith,
the following laws have been enacted...

1) The king will take the wealth of the monasteries, sell off their lands and close them. [ ]

2) All monks will worship the king as well as our Lord. [ ]

3) The Catholic religion will be replaced by the Protestant religion. [ ]

4) All children must be christened as Protestants. There will be a charge for christenings, marriages and burials. [ ]

5) Anyone who laughs out loud in front of the king will be hanged. [ ]

6) Anyone eating white bread must pay a tax to the king. [ ]

7) When a criminal is hanged his family must pay for the cost of the rope and the hangman. [ ]

Signed Thomas Cromwell
Chief minister

DID YOU KNOW…?

Tudor cooks often sewed two creatures together to make an entertaining meal. The front of a chicken and back of a pig stitched together made the legendary creature, the 'cockatrice.'

Henry VIII is famous for his huge feasts and his belt-busting eating habits. For example, in November 1531, the king held five massive banquets. Work out which of these numbered pictures would complete the banquet below.

TERRIBLE TUDOR LIFE & DEATH

Tudors weren't just terrible kings and queens. They were also ordinary people like you and me. Commoners! (Well, I'm dead common, I don't know about you!) For them, life was often grim. Nine out of ten people never made it to 40! Filthy conditions, loopy doctors and bizarre remedies kept people in terribly bad health.

Life was hard in Tudor times. There were open sewers in the streets, holes in the ground for toilets and dirty drinking water. It's amazing anyone survived! Spot ten filthy differences between the two pictures below and circle them with a pencil.

You don't like going to the doctor? You should have tried it in Tudor times! The cure was often more disgusting than the illness. Imagine you're a Tudor doctor and add the word stickers to complete these facts about horrible illnesses and their curious cures. Don't worry if you get them all wrong. Most of them wouldn't have worked anyway…

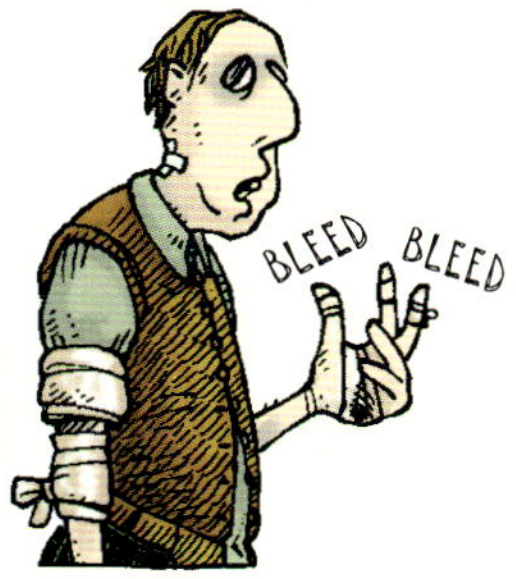

Read about these four gruesome diseases. Add the revolting stickers–A,B,C or D–careful you don't catch any nasties from them!

1) SWEATING SICKNESS
Arrived without warning in the morning or at night. It caused shivering, followed by sweating and then terrible weakness. If your body stopped sweating, then you started peeing. Many died in the first 24 hours.

2) SMALLPOX
Caused high fever and pains in the head and muscles. Sometimes your lungs filled with blood. If you survived two to five days more, a rash appeared that grew into pimples. These burst and the scabs fell off in a few weeks.

3) THE PLAGUE
Started with visibly swollen glands, then fever, chills, headache and extreme exhaustion. If it got really bad and into your lungs, you might even cough up blood and die.

4) JAIL FEVER
Caused fever and rashes all over the body. Half of those who caught it died. Caused by head lice (nits) and body lice. They like crowded, dirty conditions – there were a lot of those in Tudor times!

DID YOU KNOW…?

The Tudors didn't know that dreadful diseases were carried by fleas. Still, they weren't keen on fleas because they bit and made you itch. To get rid of them the Tudors would fill a dish with goat's blood and put it by the bed and all the fleas would come to it.

TUDOR CRIME & TERRIBLE PUNISHMENTS

Being a criminal in Tudor times wasn't very good for your health. The punishments were terrible and some even ended in death. Do *you* fancy being branded like a cow?

If you were a Justice of the Peace, your main job would be to judge cases in your local court. You'd have a lot of terrible punishments you could deal out. Here are six cases for you to try. Add the correct stickers to match the punishment to the crime – A, B, C, D, E or F.

1

BEING A TRAMP

2

A WOMAN POISONS HER HUSBAND

3

A MAN POISONS ANOTHER MAN – EVEN IF THE VICTIM DOES NOT DIE

4

LYING IN COURT "PERJURY"

5

HELPING OR SHELTERING A MURDERER

6

STEALING

If you weren't afraid of being caught – or if you were very desperate for money and food to stay alive – you might become a criminal. What sort would you like to be? A Prigger of Prancers? A Palliard? Or, maybe an Autem Mort? Read about these four Tudor criminals and add the correct picture stickers – A, B, C or D.

1

2) A HOOKER
A thief who uses a long pole with a hook on the end to "lift" other people's property.

3

4) AN AUTEM MORT
A woman who steals clothes off washing lines.

) A PALLIARD
\ beggar with dreadful ores. Could be genuine lisease, but (more often) hey'd be faked.

2

3) A PRIGGER OF PRANCERS
A person who steals horses.

4

William Harrison wrote about everyday life in Tudor England. He also looked at crime and punishment. The greatest crime in England at that time was treason – plotting against king and country. So the punishment was most horrible. Add the missing word stickers to find out what Harrison wrote...

The guilty man is drawn from the ______ to the place of ______ on a sled, where they are ______ till they be half ______ They are then taken down, and ______ into quarters; after that, their ______ are cut from their ______ and thrown into a ______ provided near at hand and within their own sight.

DID YOU KNOW...?

Mary Tudor believed it was a crime to be a Protestant. She would burn them at the stake to purify their souls. To make death quicker and kinder the victims had pouches of gunpowder strapped to their legs and arms. Instead of a slow sizzle there was just a quick bang and their bits were splattered. That was the idea, but it didn't always work.

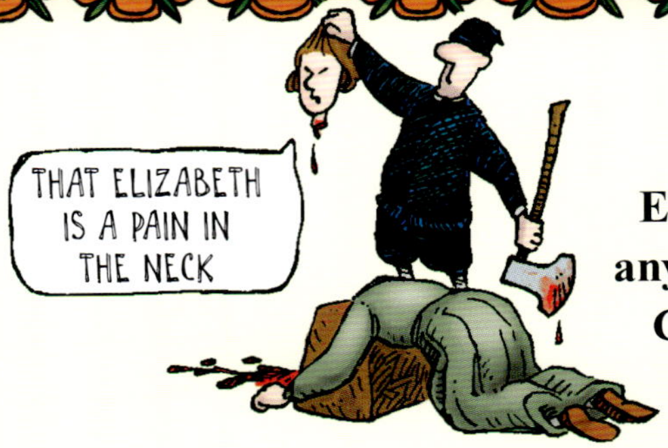

BAD QUEEN BESS

Elizabeth I had many plots against her life. She found it hard to trust anyone – even her family. Elizabeth's cousin, Mary Queen of Scots, was Catholic and a lot of English Catholics would like to have seen her on Elizabeth's throne...

Mary Queen of Scots fled from Scotland when her husband was murdered and asked her cousin Elizabeth I to protect her. Elizabeth protected Mary by having her locked away for 19 years. When Mary's Catholic friends became too dangerous then Elizabeth had the Queen of Scots beheaded. End of the Catholic plotters – end of Mary.

Read about Mary's execution and then find the words written in CAPITAL LETTERS in the puzzle. The words are written up, down, diagonally and across.

Mary didn't know she was going to DIE till the night before it happened. She stayed awake all night, writing letters and praying. By the time she got to the BLOCK she must have been ready to nod off! Three hundred people crowded into the hall to watch her EXECUTION. Mary was dressed in red, so the BLOOD wouldn't show. The axe-man's assistant held her BODY steady while the AXE fell. It missed the NECK and cut into the back of her HEAD. The second CHOP was a better shot but it still needed a bit of sawing with the axe to finish it off. Mary's HEART was removed and buried in the castle grounds and hasn't been seen since. In 1612, her son, by then James 1 of England, had her COFFIN moved to Westminster Abbey where it is today.

H	E	A	D	O	E	P	T	R	A	I
D	I	E	S	X	L	R	U	O	B	E
Q	O	C	A	F	A	D	R	G	L	H
F	M	E	X	E	C	U	T	I	O	N
B	K	C	H	O	P	J	N	P	O	B
O	B	L	O	C	K	D	V	E	D	J
D	T	R	A	X	S	Z	I	L	C	O
Y	C	O	F	F	I	N	U	T	I	K

Elizabeth was terrified of being assassinated. She banned her courtiers from wearing long cloaks because she wanted their swords uncovered and ready. Help Elizabeth find her way out of the palace garden and escape from a gang of criminals.

DID YOU KNOW…?

In Tudor England the great houses and palaces had toilets called 'jakes'. But the waste from the jakes didn't get washed away. It fell down into a pit. With hundreds of people living in a palace these pits soon filled up… and up… and up.

Elizabeth wasn't very popular when she visited other people's houses and filled up their jakes while hers were being emptied. She really was a pain in the bum! Try and work out which items you wouldn't see in a Tudor loo.

SLIMY STUART TIMES

In 1603 old Queen Elizabeth died. She was the last of the terrible Tudors. James Stuart came down from his home in Scotland to become James I of England. The Stuart family were always ducking and diving to keep out of trouble. You could never be quite sure what they were up to. In fact, they were rather slimy characters – the slimy Stuarts.

Would you like to see what those slimy Stuarts looked like? Read the vile verses below and add the correct portrait stickers to complete this royal rogues' gallery.

JAMES I

Slimy Jim, snotty Jim,
Slobbered when he drank his beer;
Hated witches, hated ciggies.
Loved to murder little deer.

CHARLES I

Charlie One, on the run;
He'd upset the Roundhead chaps.
Said that God was on his side;
God not there when Charlie axed!

CHARLES II

Charlie Two, used to woo
Lots of women, what a bloke!
Merry monarch – plague then fire,
Sent the laughter up in smoke.

JAMES II

King Jim, rather dim;
Made it clear he liked the Pope.
Britons told him, 'Push off, Jimmy!
Catholic Britain? Not a hope.'

WILLIAM

MARY

Mary big; ate like a pig;
Willie small; like her pet cat.
Smallpox killed her, as for Willie,
His horse stumbled, he went splat!

ANNE

Annie stout; feet with gout;
Food and brandy she would gorge.
Children all dead, no more Stuarts;
Throne passed on to German George.

Match the stickers to the dates to see how the slimy Stuarts ducked and dived their way through 111 years of terrifying torture and perilous plots.

1

1) 1605: An explosive plot to blow James I of England all the way back home to Scotland is discovered.

2) 1649: After Roundhead victory in a civil war, Charles I gets the chop.

2

3

3) 1660: The Stuarts return with Charles II. Ex-leader Cromwell is dug up, strung up and beheaded.

4) 1685: King Charles II apologizes to his doctors for taking so long to die, and his brother takes over.

4

5

5) 1688: James II is thrown off the throne and flees. Even his daughter, Mary, is glad to see the back of him.

6) 1702: Mary's sister, Anne, takes over the throne – she was famous for being fat, as well as having 17 children.

6

James I had a lot of Catholic enemies. One group planned to blow up the King and the Houses of Parliament on 5 November 1605. Guy Fawkes was asked to help because he was an explosives expert. Guy was discovered in the cellars on 4 November before he could set off the gunpowder. Lead the soldiers through Parliament to arrest Guy Fawkes.

DID YOU KNOW...?

The punishment for treason was horrible. The victim was hanged for a few moments, cut down and cut open. Their guts were thrown on to a fire before being beheaded and cut into quarters. Guy Fawkes had other ideas. He jumped off the ladder so that his neck broke – he was dead when they cut him open.

DEADLY STUART DAYS

People who lived through the reign of Charles II were pretty lucky – lucky that the plague didn't get them! In London alone, 100,000 people died from the Great Plague of 1665. Charles might have been a merry monarch, but it was no laughing matter for his subjects.

Most people who caught the plague died a horrible death.
The first symptoms would be swellings in the groin and the armpit.
Then the victims spat blood and in a couple of days they were dead!
How many bodies need to be taken away and dropped into a pit?

DID YOU KNOW...?

William Harvey discovered that blood 'circulates' – it goes from the heart, round the body and back to the heart again. He discovered this by cutting up corpses. After the Battle of Edgehill, he sat under a hedge and read a book to pass the time. When he grew cold … he pulled a corpse over him to keep warm!

Those poor Londoners. If the plague spared their lives, then the Great Fire probably destroyed their houses! Add the stickers to read the story usually told about the fire. Then fill in the answers in the grid. The blue column will tell you who the people of London really blamed for the fire of 1666.

A LITTLE BOY CREPT INTO THOMAS FARRINER'S BAKER'S SHOP IN PUDDING LANE. HE REACHED UP TO STEAL A ____ (1) THAT WAS COOLING BY THE WINDOW. THE ____ (2) SWUNG ROUND AND SCATTERED ____ (6) OVER THE WOODEN FLOOR. THE SHOP QUICKLY CAUGHT ____ (10) AND SOON THE WHOLE ____ (11) OF ____ (3) HOUSES WAS ____ (4) FIERCELY. SPARKS SPREAD THE FIRE ACROSS LONDON. WHEN ____ I (5) HEARD OF THE PROBLEM, HE JOINED THE FIRE-FIGHTERS. HE ENDED UP BLACKENED BY ____ (7) AND SOAKED WITH WATER. HE GAVE 100 GUINEAS TO THE BRAVE FIRE-FIGHTERS. THIS WON THE ____ (9) HUGE POPULARITY WITH THE ____ (8) OF LONDON.

If plague and fire didn't kill you in Stuart times, the doctors might! Here are six illnesses. If you were a Stuart doctor, what would you prescribe? Add the stickers to complete the horrible illnesses and their curious cures. Just don't expect them to work and *don't* try them on your friends!

CRIME AND PAINFUL PUNISHMENT

You might think there would be no one left alive after all the dreadful death and disaster, but the Stuarts had a vivid imagination when it came to curious crimes and painful punishments.

If you wanted to survive in Stuart Britain, you had to know who was out to get you. Can you add the correct stickers to match the criminals to their methods and their crimes?

THIS CRIMINAL	WOULD ...	AND ...
DARKMAN'S BUDGE 		LET IN A GANG. 
	WALK PAST YOUR HEDGE 	
SNUDGE 		STEAL FROM IT. 
	PLAY CARDS WITH YOU 	
FOOTPAD 		ROB STAGE COACHES. 

DID YOU KNOW...?

The people of Halifax had an early guillotine which released a blade by pulling on a rope. The crowd all pulled together, so no single person was to blame for the criminal's death. But, if the thief had stolen a cow, for example, then a cow was tied to the rope and driven away. So a cow could guillotine a man!

The Stuart time was one of the classic ages of the highwayman. Stage coach journeys had begun. One man called William Nevison once rode from York to London in just 16 hours to avoid being convicted of a robbery. Add the stickers in the correct order, working from left to right, to read about this great feat…

Read about these five potty punishments and add the correct picture stickers.

1) THUMBEKINS
Your thumbs are placed in a vice which is tightened until you talk.

1

2

2) DRUNKARD'S CLOAK
You are placed in a barrel with a hole in the top and bottom, and a hole in each side for your arms. You then walk around the streets.

3) BRANKS
You wear an iron mask with a spike that goes into your mouth. A punishment for women who nag or talk too much!

3

4

4) CROPPING
Your head is put in a pillory and your ears are nailed to the wood. Your ears are then cut off and left fastened to the pillory.

5) REPENTANCE STOOL
You sit down in a church while the priest tells everyone what a disgusting person you are.

5

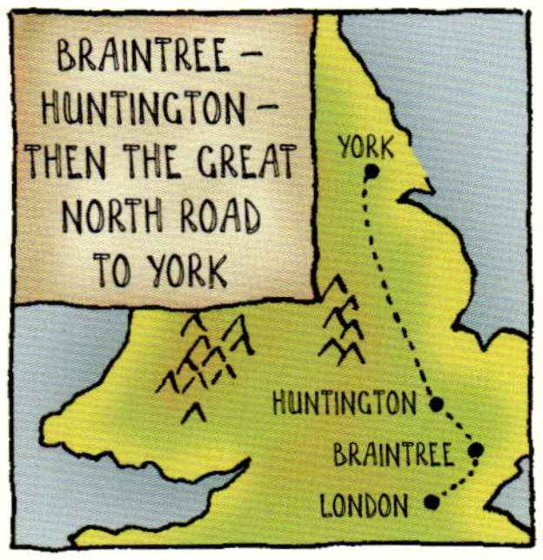

STRANGE STUART FADS

If you were invited to eat at an upper-class house in Stuart times, you'd eat off fine silver and gold plates ... but you'd be expected to take your own spoon! When the Stuarts did get round to forks, they used them to pick their teeth! They also ate meat with their fingers and threw bones on the floor. Everyone used the same bowl of water to wash their fingers and rinse their spoons in!

The Stuarts discovered lots of new food and drink ideas that we still have today. Work out which of the lettered pictures are part of the image. Which of the labelled things would you have seen in Stuart Britain?

DID YOU KNOW...?

Although James I put large taxes on tobacco, some people, including herbalist Nicholas Culpeper, thought tobacco was good for you! If you rubbed tobacco juice into a child's head, they thought it would kill the lice in it.

The Stuarts ate a lot of meat. Kitchen boys had the hard job of turning the meat over an open fire. Inventors came up with a couple of devices. One was a large 'hamster-wheel'. Instead of a hamster, you put a dog inside. As the dog walked forward, the meat turned. Spot six differences between the two pictures and circle them with a pencil.

The Stuarts loved going to the fair with all of its weird fun – rope dancers, bull baiting and ... toad-eating! Men pretended to eat a toad. They acted as if they were dying, then took a 'miracle cure'. The crowds believed everything they saw – and then bought the 'medicine'. Add the missing stickers to read these horrible toad-eating facts.

1) Some toad-eaters trained their ______ by putting them on their ______ so that they didn't get excited by the idea and sweat poison.

2) A young man who was fit, and who had just eaten a good meal, could probably ______ swallowing a toad. He might get stomach and ______ pains though!

3) When a toad is attacked it ______ out a deadly milky poison. A dog trying to eat a toad will start ______ at the mouth.

4) In Stuart times a new word was invented for creeps – ______ .

5) There is a record of Roman women using toad ______ to kill their husbands. They threw a toad into ______ water – the poison rose to the surface. It was skimmed off and fed to the husband.

STUART CHILDREN

Many babies died in Stuart times because families didn't understand about deadly germs. For every 100 people who died, 40 were under two years. Some rich parents couldn't be bothered with wailing and whingeing babies. They sent the baby away to nurses in the country until the child was old enough to walk and talk. They did visit it from time to time though.

Would you like to have been a child in Stuart times? If you were the child of a strict Puritan, then you could have been stuck with a rotten religious name. Which of the following nasty names were really given to nippers? Answer true or false and add the correct stickers.

1) Silence		6) Sorry-for-Sin	
2) Helpless		7) Good-for-Nothing	
3) Forsaken		8) Posthuma	
4) Ugly		9) Discipline	
5) Hide-and-Seek		10) Decrease	

Find the words in CAPITALS in the wordsearch. They are written forwards, backwards, up, down, diagonally and across.

A	P	B	O	T	M	T
T	E	O	C	A	O	R
S	T	Y	S	G	N	O
W	T	S	D	N	E	U
I	I	G	R	I	Y	S
T	C	O	A	C	P	E
C	O	W	C	N	E	R
H	A	M	O	A	G	S
M	T	R	A	D	E	S

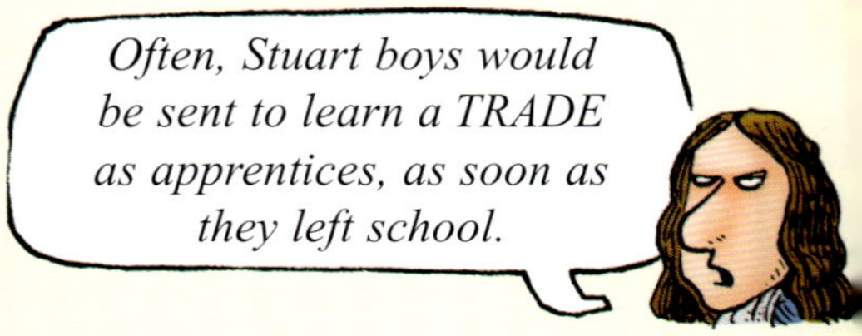

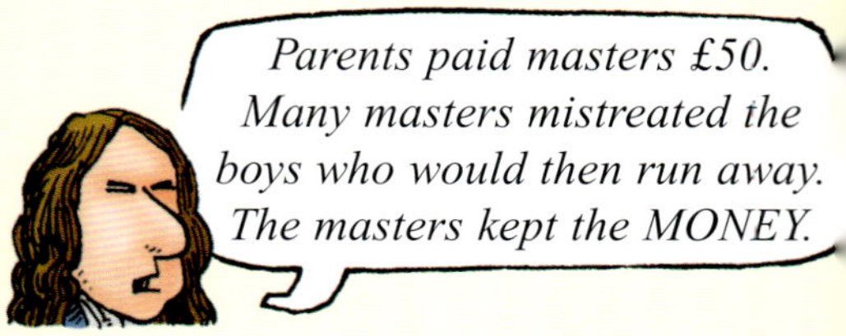

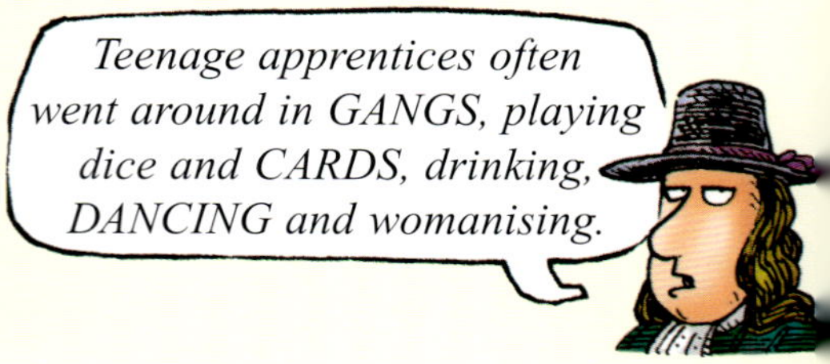

If you think school uniform is a bore, what would you have worn in Stuart times? Parents liked to dress up their children to show other people how wealthy they were. Use the stickers to dress these privileged Stuart children.

DID YOU KNOW...?

Children didn't stand much of a chance in Stuart times – even the rich ones. Queen Anne had 17 babies and 16 died. Only William survived infancy ... then he died at the age of 11. Anne died in 1714 – she had grown so fat her coffin was almost square! Without a Stuart heir, the Hanovers were invited to take over the throne. Goodbye slimy Stuarts. Hello horrible Hanovers.

ANSWERS

Pages 4-5 ROTTEN ROMAN RULERS

Rome had its fair share of rotten…

Missing words in the correct order: SMASH, LEG, RULE, HORSE, WIFE, DROWN, MOTHER, CORPSE, RIVER TIBER, EATING, CHEESE, COBWEB, CHICKEN.

Julius Caesar was a brilliant…

Augustus Caesar was a…

1 = True **2** = False **3** = False

4 = True **5** = False **6** = True

2) The doctor was part of a plot to kill Claudius. He tickled his throat with a poisoned feather.
3) Nero wasn't in Rome when the fire started.
4) Gordian hung himself with his belt when he heard his son had died fighting for him.

Pages 6-7 GRUESOME GAMES

People believed that the souls of the dead…

3, **5** and **6** are not part of the Colosseum.

Fighters became known as gladiators.

ANDABATAE

SAGITTARII

RETIARII

DIMACHERI

SECUTORES

LAQUEATORES

Gladiators wore armour…

H	I	A	P	A	R	M	A
A	S	U	I	D	A	L	G
S	V	A	T	H	U	F	A
T	B	N	A	E	L	A	G
A	Y	I	O	C	Q	S	O
O	T	C	J	F	I	L	C
C	G	S	E	A	M	S	R
R	M	A	N	I	C	A	E
E	H	F	L	U	R	A	C
A	O	C	T	E	P	I	T
A	T	U	L	N	R	A	C
T	M	A	N	X	A	U	I
I	A	C	U	L	U	M	S

Pages 8-9 FEARSOME FIGHTERS

Not everyone thought that…

Missing words in the correct order: SPORT, FIGHTERS, BODIES, ESCAPE, DEFEATED, MURDERERS, WRONG.

Gladiators were supposed…

1

2

3

4

5

6

7

8

Want some fun in ancient Rome?

C matches the picture in the middle.

Pages 10-11 ROTTEN ROMAN ARMY

To conquer another…

Find the stickers to complete…

The word BATTLE can be seen **15** times.

B	A	T	T	L	E	T	A	B
A	E	L	T	T	A	B	B	B
T	A	T	L	L	B	A	A	E
T	L	E	T	B	A	T	T	L
L	T	T	A	L	T	T	T	T
E	L	T	T	L	T	L	L	T
T	E	T	E	A	L	E	E	A
T	E	L	T	T	B	L	A	B
A	L	A	T	A	A	T	T	E
B	A	B	E	T	B	T	B	L
A	A	L	A	A	A	A	A	T
T	T	L	T	T	A	B	T	T
T	T	T	A	B	T	B	T	A
L	L	A	L	B	T	L	L	B
E	E	B	A	T	T	L	E	E
B	A	E	L	T	T	A	B	B

When the Romans captured…

PICTURES OF COMPLETED DOGS

You did not want to be an enemy of Rome.

1 = B **2** = C **3** = A

Pages 12-13 ROTTEN ROMAN PUNISHMENT

In AD 64 there was a huge fire…

 = dogs  = crosses  = flames

 = torches  = circus  = chariot

In the reign of…

1 = C **2** = B **3** = A

Romans often tried…

Can you add the correct stickers…

1 = F **2** = D **3** = A **4** = E **5** = C **6** = B

Pages 14-15
VICIOUS VIKING TIMES

So why did the Vikings leave their homeland...

1 = True **2** = False **3** = False **4** = True **5** = True
6 = True **7** = True **8** = False – Vikings only had horns on their helmets for important ceremonies.

The Vikings were a tough lot in a violent...

1 = C 2 = A 3 = B 4 = D

Some people argue the Vikings were a loveable...

1 = C 2 = A 3 = B

Pages 16-17
VICIOUS VIKING INVADERS

The Viking ships are admired for their low...

The Vikings had strict rules when sailing the...

1 = D 2 = B 3 = C 4 = D

Imagine crossing the freezing North Sea in an...

Boat 1 = England **Boat 2** = Iceland **Boat 3** = Ireland
Boat 4 = Greenland **Boat 5** = France **Boat 6** = Newfoundland

Pages 18-19 LIVE LIKE A VIKING

Vikings ate cheese, smoked meats and...

Life wasn't easy for the women and children left...

Missing words in the correct order: HAIR, NITS, RAID, FARMING, HOUSEWORK, SWIM, WEAPONS, MOSS.

Life was horrible for the Viking slaves...

JOBS FOR THE BOYS:
- DIG PEAT FOR FUEL
- HERD PIGS AND GOATS
- SPREAD MANURE
- BUILD WALLS

JOBS FOR THE GIRLS:
- MILK COWS AND GOATS
- GRIND CORN BY HAND
- MAKE CHEESE
- WASH
- COOK

Pages 20-21
GRUESOME GODS AND SHOCKING SAGAS

Christianity did not appeal to your average...

1 = E 2 = C 3 = D 4 = A 5 = B

You may think the stories you heard as a...

Unscrambled words in the correct order: TROUBLE, HARMING, REVENGE, SEWING, MISTLETOE, PUNISH, GUTS.

Viking poems gloried in death and destruction.

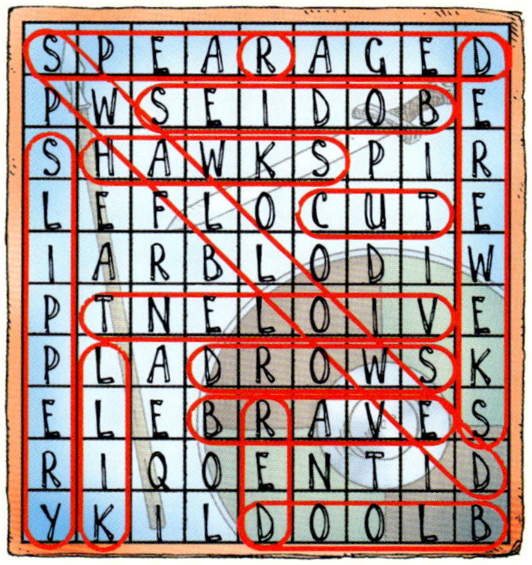

Pages 22-23 KING ALFRED THE GREAT

One such story tells of Alfred inventing the...

Boxes 2, 3 and 4 are part of the scene.

King Alfred made a book of laws for the...

1 = D 2 = C 3 = A 4 = B

If you didn't like Alfred's law, you could move to...

Pages 24-25
THE AWFUL AZTECS

When the wandering Aztecs first arrived in...

1) = C 2) = D 3) = F 4) = A 5) = B 6) = E

The city of Teotihuacan was massive and...

Missing words in the correct order: MUDDY, SACRIFICES, NASTY, CHILDREN, NECK, GROW, RATTLESNAKE, PIERCED, DRILLED, SQUAWK, BATTLES, SKINS, VICTIMS, DREADFUL.

Life wasn't as hard for the emperor...

The emperor spoke to the SUN GOD.

Pages 26-27 LIVE LIKE AN AZTEC

If you wanted the gods to bring you rain...

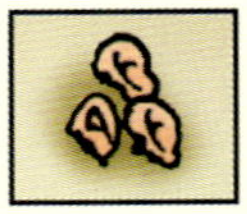
= ears

= fire

= smoke

= tied

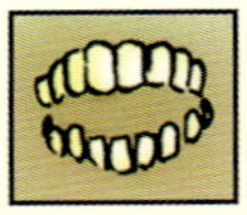
= teeth

= jar

So you survive an Aztec childhood...

If you were an Aztec boy...

1) = D 2) = H 3) = G
4) = F 5) = I 6) = B
7) = E 8) = A 9) = C

1) You must use an old woman as the messenger to carry your proposal.

2) Don't bother asking the girl herself because you don't need her permission.

6) The marriage takes place at night, that's why there is a torch-lit procession.

Pages 28-29
FUNNY FOOD AND GORY GAMES

Thanks to the Aztecs, we...

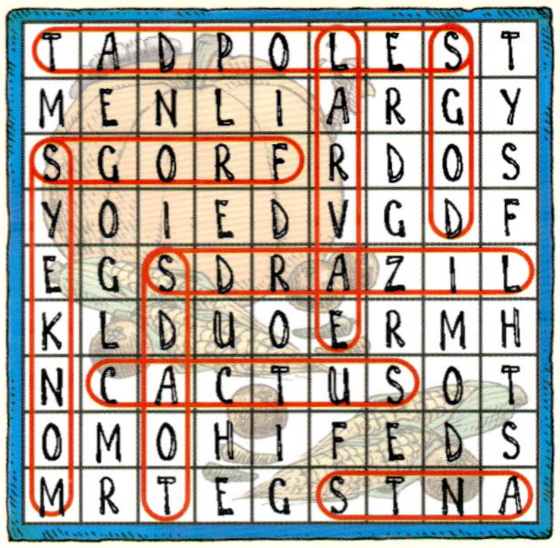

So that's the food taken care of, but what did the...

Missing words in the correct order: HONEY, BACTERIA, MOUTHS, SPAT, BOWL, FROTH, BUBBLE, TEETH.

The Aztecs enjoyed playing a jolly little...

Pages 30-31 SCARY SACRIFICES

Health warning: if you are sickened at the sight of...

2 = E 3 = A 4 = D 5 = B 6 = C

The Aztecs' favourite sacrifices...

1) = D 2) = C 3) = E 4) = A 5) = B

Some victims were sacrificed...

Boxes 1, 2, 5, 7 and 9 are part of the picture.

Pages 32-33
THE CUNNING CONQUISTADORS

See what fantastic facts you...

1) = False 2) = True 3) = True
4) = False 5) = True 6) = True
7) = False 8) = False 9) = False
10) = True 11) = True 12) = False

2) That's what the Spanish soldiers said when they fought against them. Before the Spanish arrived the Aztecs did NOT cut off horses' heads because there were no horses in Mexico.

4 & 12) Warriors believed that dying in battle was a wonderful thing. They believed that they were immediately turned into hummingbirds and hummed off to join the sun god in heaven.

6) Young men had to leave some of their hair long–a disgraceful thing which told everyone that they weren't a real man yet.

9) They did wear armour, but it wasn't made of metal because they didn't have steel. It was a padded coat, soaked in salt water to make it hard.

Aztec warriors were led by an emperor...

1 = B 2 = D 3 = E 4 = C 5 = A

The invading Spanish were shocked to...

There are 31 skulls in the first column, 47 in the second and 58 in the third: 31 + 47 + 58 = 136 x 1000 = The Spanish discovered 136,000 skulls.

Pages 34-35 DARK KNIGHTS

Match the correct picture stickers to the…

1) = H	2) = C	3) = G	4) = A	5) = B
6) = J	7) = D	8) = F	9) = E	10) = I

Knights had more rules than your…

Unscrambled words in the correct order: MONEY, FRIENDS, OFTEN, READY, BATTLE, BRAVE, HUNTING, INSULTED

But, above all else, a knight…

Jaufre DIED on the spot. The only man ever to have been killed by beauty. Every knight believed he was that much in love with his lady, BUT … this book is a horrible history, and the horribly sad truth is Jaufre did NOT die in the arms of the Countess of Tripoli. He lived on until he died of old age.

Pages 36-37 KNIGHTLY ORDERS

These days only the monarch of the…

Correct order of the missing pictures is: C, D, G, E, A, F and B. Today, members of the Order of the Garter have the words, 'Shame on those who think this is shameful', on their badge – except it is written in medieval French: *Honi soit qui mal y pense*.

If the Queen won't make you…

The knight is from the Order of the Bath, founded between 1399 and 1413.

Pages 38-39 TERRIFIC TOURNAMENTS

Tournaments took war and…

How did you score? Count up the number of 'yes' ticks you have.
7–10 yes ticks: you're a wimp. Forget about becoming a knight and take up basket-weaving instead.
3–6 ticks: feeble. You would not last very long in a tournament.
2 ticks: you're a knight … if you ticked the correct two rules, numbers 5 and 10.

Tournaments were all about winning…

Knight A's prize is a velvet cap, knight B's prize is some talking parrots, knight C is going to win a silver lion and knight D's prize is a bear.

As well as tournaments there were…

Pages 40-41 CRUEL CRUSADES

In 1095, Pope Urban II decided it was time…

Missing words in the correct order: NAVELS, DEATH, ORGANS, DRAG, FLOG, KILL, ENTRAILS, SHOOT, BARE, ATTACK, CUT

Of course, the Pope…

The stories the Pope said were…

1 = True	2 = True	3 = True	4 = False	5 = True
6 = False	7 = True	8 = False	9 = False	10 = False

4) The priest's name was Peter the Hermit. He got peasants to believe that if enough pilgrims reached Jerusalem then Christ would return.
6) The Crusaders ate leather and stewed tree bark.
8) They reached Jerusalem on 15 June 1099.
9) The Turks put the gold in their mouths. When they were cornered they swallowed the gold like human piggy banks.
10) Pope Urban II was dead when the victory news was received in Rome. He died just two days before the news arrived. The capture of Jerusalem did not end the Crusades, as the Crusaders wanted to get rid of the Muslims from the whole region, not just from Jerusalem. This desire led to other crusades. But by 1291, nearly 200 years after the First Crusade, the Christians lost their last city in the Holy Land.

Pages 42-43 CRAZY CASTLE LIFE

Most castles had a dreadful dungeon – an underground…

1 = The Gauntlets	2 = The Boot	3 = The Rack
4 = Skeffington's gyves	5 = Thumbscrews	

In 1066, when William the Conqueror invaded…

Boxes 1, 2 and 5 are part of the picture.

Castles were really fun places to live…

1 = C	2 = E	3 = D	4 = A	5 = B

Pages 44-45

WHAT IS A TERRIBLE TUDOR?

Confused by which monarch is which?

Henry VII

Henry VIII

Edward VI

Mary I

Elizabeth I

Henry VIII was fat, ruthless and cruel.

1) 1509

2) 1536

3) 1536

4) 1547

Being the wife of Henry VIII...

1 = girl (Mary I)/divorced
2 = girl (Elizabeth I)/beheaded
3 = boy (Edward VI)/died
4 = no children/divorced
5 = no children/beheaded
6 = no children/survived

Pages 46-47 HORRIBLE HENRY VIII

Henry wanted power over everything...

1 = YEA **2** = NAY **3** = YEA **4** = YEA **5** = NAY **6** = YEA **7** = NAY

When Henry saw a picture of Anne of Cleves...

Henry accused her of being a horse.

Henry VIII is famous for his huge...

2, **4**, **6** and **7** would complete the banquet

Pages 48-49

TERRIBLE TUDOR LIFE & DEATH

Life was hard in Tudor...

You don't like going to...

1) Cover the body with tobacco juice to cure fleas.
2) Swallow nine lice mixed with a little ale each morning for a week to cure jaundice or 'bad liver'.
3) Crush garlic, rub it in the head and wash in vinegar to cure baldness.
4) Find the gall of a hare and the grease of a fox, warm the mixture and place in the ear to cure deafness.
5) Boil a red-haired dog in oil, add worms, pig's marrow and herbs. Make a mixture and put it on the affected area to cure gout.

Read about these four gruesome...

1 = C **2** = A **3** = D **4** = B

Pages 50-51 TUDOR CRIME & TERRIBLE PUNISHMENTS

If you were a Justice of the Peace...

1 = C **2** = A **3** = E **4** = F **5** = D **6** = B

If you weren't afraid of being caught...

1 = B **2** = A **3** = C **4** = D

William Harrison wrote about...

Missing words in the correct order: PRISON, EXECUTION, HANGED, DEAD, CUT, BOWELS, BODIES, FIRE

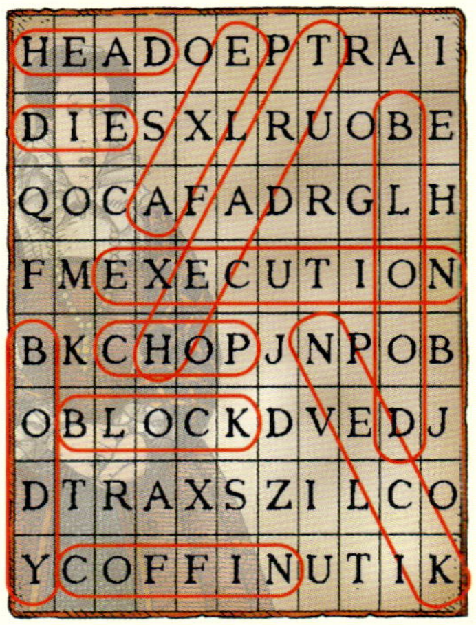

Pages 52-53

BAD QUEEN BESS

Read about Mary's...

Elizabeth was terrified of being assassinated...

In Tudor England the great houses...

You wouldn't find an air freshener, toilet brush or toilet paper in a Tudor loo. Queen Elizabeth's godson, Sir John Harrington, invented the first flushing toilet. The Queen was so impressed, she had them fitted in all of her palaces.

Pages 54-55 SLIMY STUART TIMES

Would you like to see what those…

James I

Charles I

Charles II

James II

William

Mary

Anne

Match the stickers to the…

1) 1605

2) 1649

3) 1660

4) 1685

5) 1688

6) 1702

James I had a lot of Catholic…

Pages 56-57 DEADLY STUART DAYS

Most people who caught the…

There are 45 bodies in the picture.

Those poor Londoners. If the…

1 = LOAF **2** = BAKER **3** = WOODEN **4** = BURNING
5 = CHARLES **6** = ASHES **7** = SMOKE **8** = PEOPLE
9 = KING **10** = FIRE **11** = STREET

The people of London blamed FRENCH SPIES. Whenever they met a Frenchman in the street, they would attack him.

If plague and fire didn't kill you in…

- Scratch your gum with a nail then drive the nail in an oak tree to cure toothache.
- Cut a pigeon in half and place one half on each foot to cure fever.
- Write the word 'Veronica' on your left thumb to cure heavy bleeding.
- Eat snails boiled in milk – add a few chopped worms to cure lung disease.
- Place a cold marble stone on the stomach to cure colic.
- Take two fish, split them open and place on the feet for 12 hours to cure liver disease.

Pages 58-59 CRIME AND PAINFUL PUNISHMENT

If you wanted to survive in Stuart Britain…

A **Darkman's Budge** would climb into your house and let in a gang.
A **Snow dropper** would walk past your hedge and steal your washing.
A **Snudge** would hide in your house till dark and steal from it.
A **Thimble-Rigger** would play cards with you and cheat you out of money.
A **Footpad** would wait by the roadside and rob stage coaches.

The Stuart time…

Read about these five potty…

1 = C **2** = E **3** = A **4** = D **5** = B

Pages 60-61 STRANGE STUART FADS

The Stuarts discovered lots of…

Boxes B, C, F, G and H are part of the picture.

You would have seen tea, eating with forks, pineapples, coffee, ice-cream, bananas and drinking chocolate in Stuart Britain.

The Stuarts ate a lot of…

The Stuarts loved going to…

Missing words in the correct order:
TOADS, TONGUES, SURVIVE, HEAD, SQUEEZES, FOAMING, 'TOAD-EATER', POISON, BOILING.

Pages 62-63 STUART CHILDREN

Would you like to have been a child…

1 = True **2** = True **3** = True **4** = False **5** = False
6 = True **7** = False **8** = True **9** = True **10** = False

Add the stickers…

A	P	B	O	T	M	T
T	E	O	C	A	O	R
S	T	Y	S	G	N	O
W	T	S	D	N	E	U
I	I	G	R	I	Y	S
T	C	O	A	C	P	E
C	O	W	C	N	E	R
H	A	M	O	A	G	S
M	T	R	A	D	E	S

If you think school uniform…

HORRIBLE HISTORIES

AWESOME ACTIVITY BOOK

TERRY DEARY

With over 200 stickers, the Awesome Activity Book will keep you (and your mummy) wrapped up for hours!

Make sure you've got the whole horrible lot!

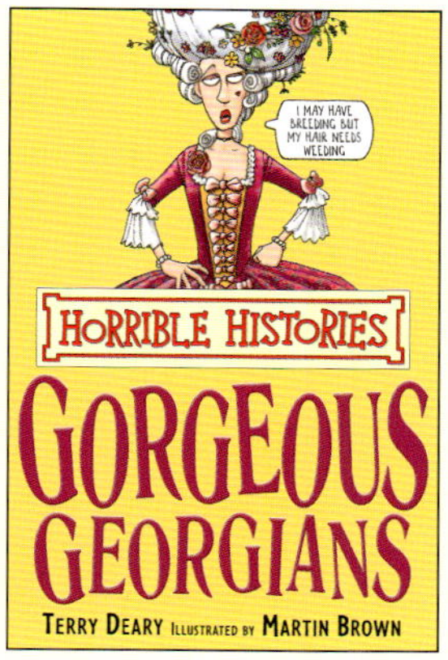

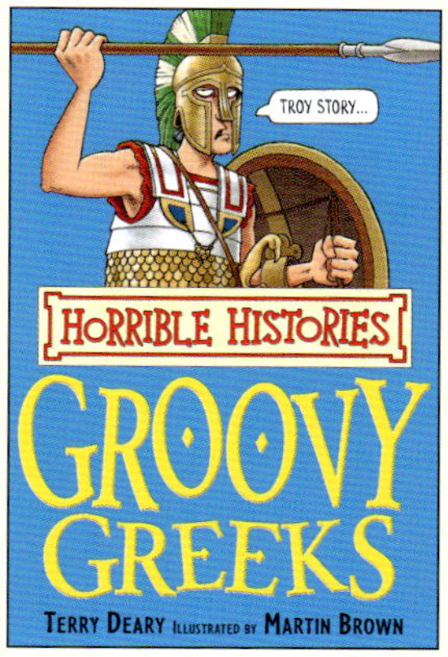

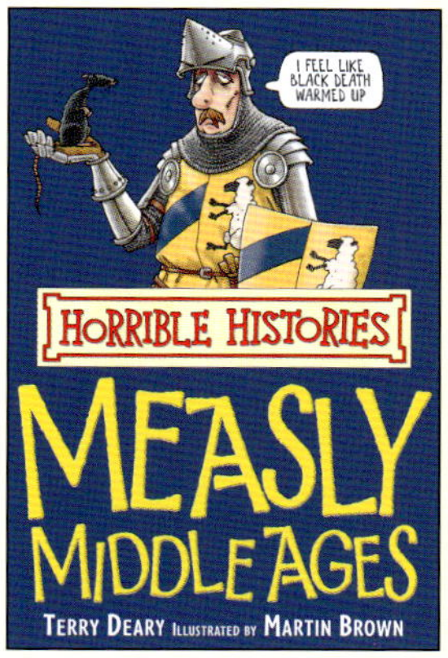

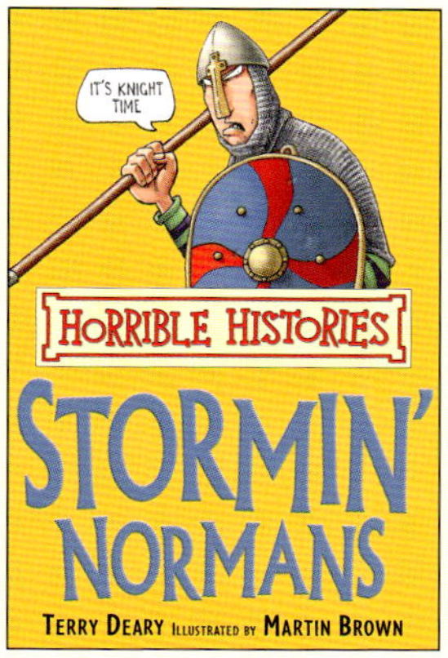

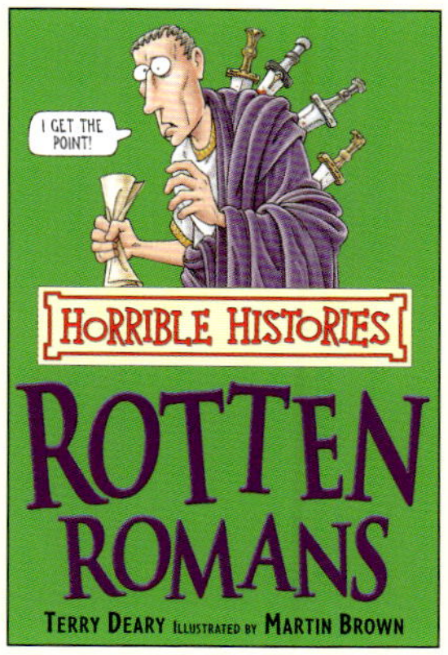

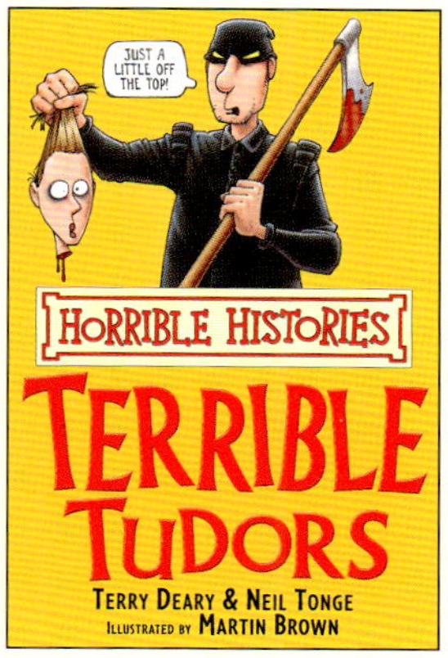

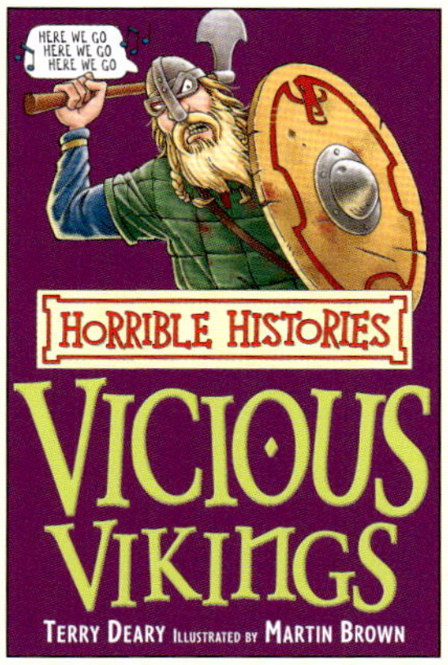

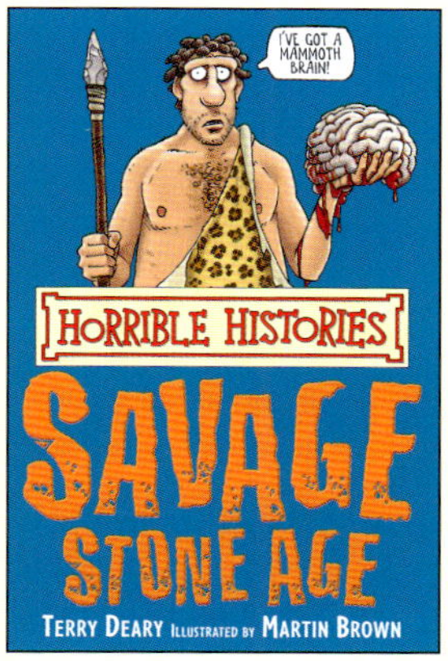

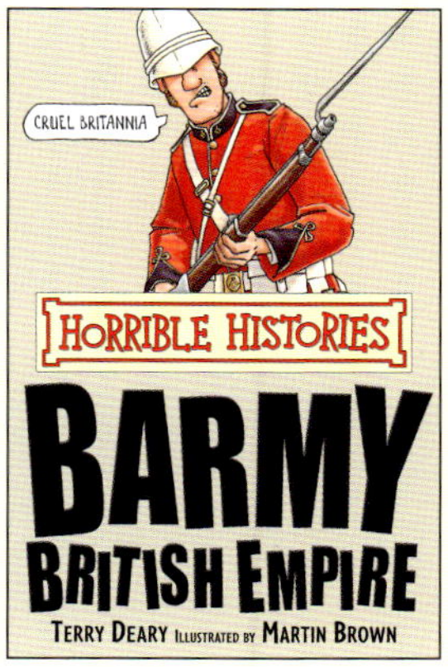

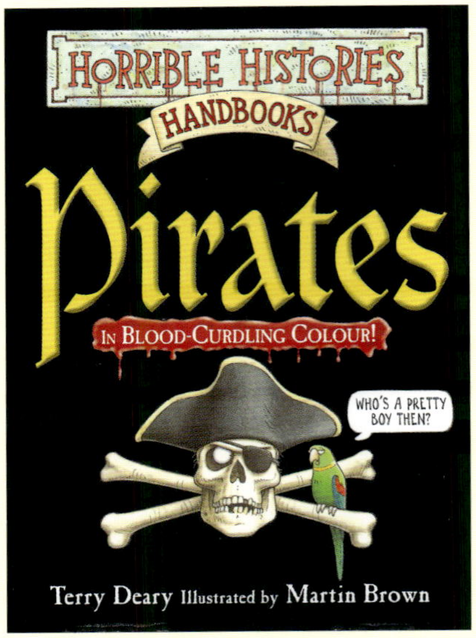

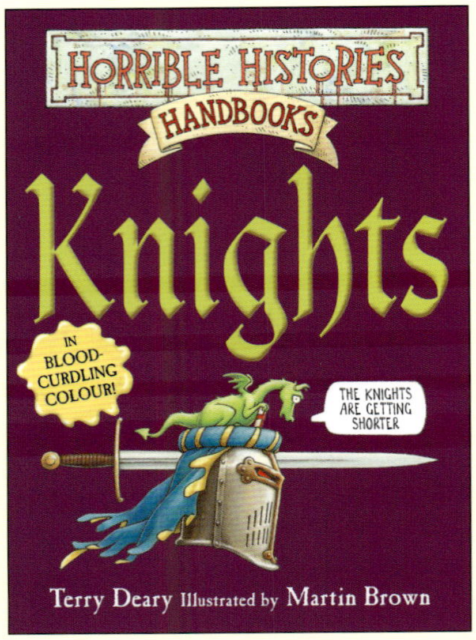

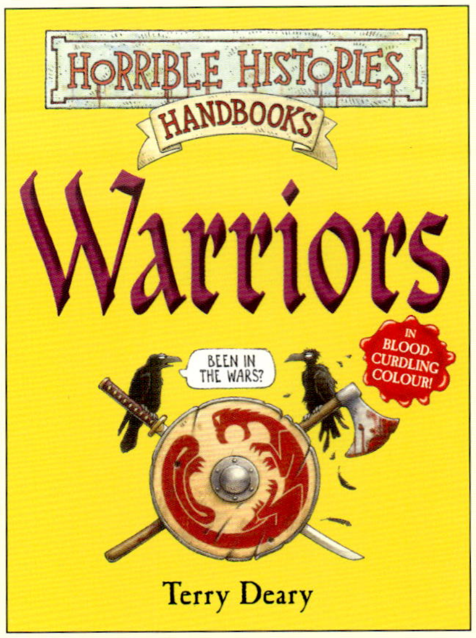

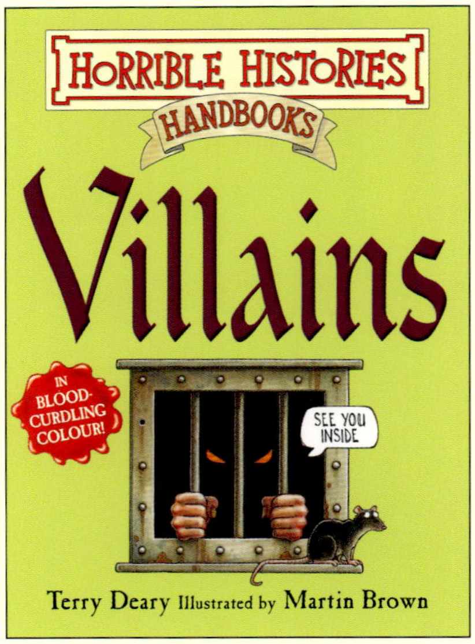

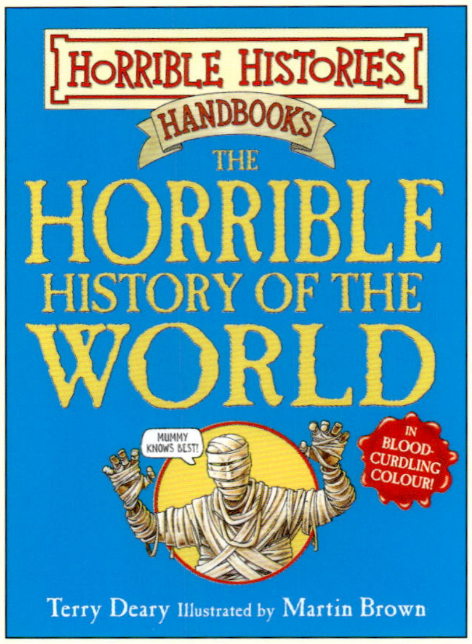

Don't miss these horribly handy handbooks for all the gore and more!